# ***IMPORTANT***

Dear Customer,

Here is your copy of **'Goodbye, My Friend'** by Andr~
We trust it will provide you with everything you need to
memorable production.

Please read carefully the **Performance Licence Application**
details on page 2 of this booklet. For any performance of drama,
narrative and dialogue from published materials like this you are
legally required to purchase a valid performance licence **from the
publishers** – in this case Edgy Productions. This is standard
practice. Please note that **local authority issued licences, PRS,
CCLI, MCPS or equivalent licences do not cover these
performances.**

If it is your intention to only use this material within the classroom
as a learning activity, or to just sing the songs only in assemblies
(using overhead transparencies) and not to an audience of
parents, no fee is due.* In these circumstances you are covered by
those licences mentioned above. **If, however you intend to make
photocopies for any of these purposes, a fee is payable.**

Please photocopy then complete the form on page 2, and post us
your performance details (with fee if applicable) no later than 28
days before your first performance, and a licence will be issued.
Alternatively, you can apply for your licence online, by visiting our
website **www.edgyproductions.com**

Should you have any questions regarding this matter, or the
staging of 'Goodbye, My Friend', please get in touch and we will be
happy to help in any way we can.

* Where no fee is due you are still obliged to return a Performance Application form –
see Page 2

**\*\*\*\*\*\*\*\*\*\*\*\*\*\*\*\* *IMPORTANT* \*\*\*\*\*\*\*\*\*\*\*\*\*\*\*\***

# PERFORMANCE LICENCE APPLICATION FORM

For **any** performance of **any part of the script** of 'Goodbye, My Friend' a valid performance licence from Edgy Productions **must** be held. Please note, **your PRS, MCPS, CCLI licence (or similar) does not cover you for performances of the script of this production**. Please ensure you complete and return the relevant sections of this form, along with the fee where applicable, at least 28 days before your first performance. You can also apply online at www.edgyproductions.com
For performances where an admission charge is made, a form will be sent which you should return with 10% of the takings (plus VAT @ 17.5%) within 28 days of the final performance.

By ticking please indicate which performance licence applies to you, and send a photocopy of this form along with the fee (where applicable) to:
**Permissions, Edgy Productions, 4 Queen Street, Uppingham, Rutland LE15 9QR**

A copy of your Performance Licence will be posted to you upon receipt of payment.

| Licence 1 | Licence 2 | Licence 3 |
|---|---|---|
| **For up to 5 performances in one year, of only the songs, within school, to only staff and children of that school, at which no admission is charged, and for which no rehearsal photocopies are made:** | **For up to 5 performances in one year, of the script and/or songs, to the public/parents, at which no admission is charged:** | **For up to 5 performances in one year, of the script and/or songs, to the public/parents, at which an admission charge is made:** |
| **NO FEE** ☐ | **£26.50** *(inc VAT)* ☐ | **£26.50** *(inc VAT)* ☐ <br> + 10% of takings *(plus VAT @ 17.5%)* |
| **This licence allows only the use of handwritten transparencies of songs. No photocopies allowed** | **This licence includes permission to photocopy the script and songs** | **This licence includes permission to photocopy the script and songs** |

*Writers rely on payments from public performances for their livelihoods. Please ensure they receive their dues.*

NAME...........................SCHOOL.................................................

ADDRESS ...................................................................................

TEL.......................... EMAIL...................................................

Number of performances......... Dates of performances from ............. to .............

I enclose a cheque for £26.50 *(if applicable)* payable to Edgy Productions Ltd ☐ Tick one box
Please send me an invoice for £26.50 *(if applicable)* to be paid within 30 days ☐

*Note: If you are applying for this licence within 14 days of purchasing your booklet and CD, you are eligible for a 20% discount. Please contact us for details.*

*YOU CAN NOT RECORD YOUR PERFORMANCE/S AND SELL OR GIVE AWAY VIDEO, DVD, CD OR CASSETTE DUPLICATIONS, WITHOUT PURCHASING A FURTHER LICENCE FROM EDGY PRODUCTIONS. PLEASE CONTACT US FOR DETAILS. SHOULD YOU MAKE AND DISTRIBUTE RECORDINGS WITHOUT THIS LICENCE YOU WILL BE IN BREACH OF COPYRIGHT LAW.*

# *Characters and plot overview by scene*

Here is a scene-by-scene overview of the characters and storylines. It is unlikely you will have the time or inclination to perform every scene and song, so below is a guide to help you choose those you want to include in your production. Continuity scripts have been written specifically to introduce and link each scene, though you may wish to personalise this aspect of the show with your own memoirs of the specific areas of school life covered in the scene.

## *All continuity Scenes*
### *Characters*
**4 children**

## *Scene 1 – page 6*
### *(associated song – Monday Morning Routine)*
Enjoy the chaos that is a Monday morning in the classroom! With registration, lunch money to collect, mums wanting 'a word', lost bags, late children, and lots more, will our over-wrought teacher remember it's her turn to take assembly?
### *Characters*
**Teacher, 12 children, a mum**

## *Scene 2 – page 12*
### *(associated song – Hey TA!)*
Discover just how indispensable our teaching assistants are, as a hapless teacher struggles to make a confused class understand some simple maths! In a hilarious bit of role reversal find out who really wears the trousers (or should that be rubber gloves) in the classroom!
### *Characters*
**Teacher, teaching assistant, 6 Children**

## *Scene 3 – page 17*
### *(associated song – PE Nightmare)*
See how two very different approaches to teaching PE can lead to some very amusing results! As one teacher tries to squeeze every last drop from the kids, the other is just happy to be outside in the sun with a bottle of factor 10!
### *Characters*
**2 teachers, 14 long-jumping children**

## *Scene 4 – page 22*
### *(associated song – School Trip Boogie)*
After the back seat scramble, the umpteenth head count, the complaints of a grumpy driver, travel sickness and countless verses of 'The Wheels On The Bus', will the class get to the zoo in time for the historic birth of a baby panda?
### *Characters*
**Teacher, 2 adult helpers, bus driver, 8 children**

## *Scene 5 – page 27*
### *(associated song – SATs Blues)*
Find out what goes through the minds of three very different children as they sit down to do a science SAT paper. From blind panic, to the creative use of a mirror for cheating, it goes to prove that doing a test is anything but boring!
### *Characters*
**3 children**

### Scene 6 – page 31
*(associated song – New School Dinner)*

What has been the real outcome of Jamie Oliver's campaign for improved school dinners? Decide whether it really is a blessing, as these children choose from a Michelin-star menu, under the watchful eye of a front-of-house team who will not accept bad manners or sloppy dining habits!

**Characters**
**4 cooks, 5 dinner ladies, 8 children**

### Scene 7 – page 37
*(associated song – The Lunchtime Frontline)*

Here's a group of fearless lunchtime supervisors in a gritty, real-life TV documentary. Join them as they patrol the playground and field, fighting crime in one of the toughest environments imaginable!

**Characters**
**Narrator, Betty, Doreen, Gladys, Phyllis, Audrey, 10 children**

### Scene 8 – page 41
*(associated song – Mr Fixit)*

Meet Jim Fixit, the loveable school caretaker, who, along with his skilled team, will try to come to the aid of anyone in school with a maintenance problem. With requests ranging from fixing the bell to ring 15 minutes early, to oiling the secretary's swivel chair so she can spin round faster, he has his work cut out!

**Characters**
**Jim Fixit, Chippy, Sparky, Bricky, Pipes**

### Scene 9 – page 45
*(associated song – Ride Our Bikes)*

In a drive to re-introduce traditional playground games, and break free from the shackles of 'Health & Safety', witness the hilarious consequences of the school's Conker Tournament!

**Characters**
**4 parents, 4 children, Headteacher**

### Scene 10 – page 50
*(associated song – Silent Night? Not Quite!)*

If you only perform one scene, it has to be this one! Watch in horror (and delight!) as the infant nativity play descends into chaos! With decapitated dolls, a flattened donkey, fighting wise-men, angels with stage fright, and a teacher about to explode, this is five minutes that will bring the house down!

**Characters**
**Teacher, 3 angels, Gabriel, Mary, Joseph, donkey** (both ends), **innkeeper, shepherds, wise men**

### Scene 11 – page 55
*(associated song – Arty Party!)*

With only minutes in which to produce some artwork to show in 'Good Work' assembly, and not wanting to make a mess, the teacher (and her class) are really up against it! 'Painting-by-numbers' has never been more appropriate!

**Characters**
**Teacher, 6 children**

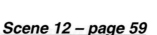

### *Scene 12 – page 59*

*(associated song – I Wish I Was An Infant Again)*

Why do infants seem to get such an easy ride? Afternoon play times, shoe laces tied for them, lots of playing in the sand......? All is not as it seems, as we discover just what fools the 'littlies' are taking us for!

### *Characters*
**8 infants, 2 parents, teacher, teaching assistant**

### *Scene 13 – page 64*

*(associated song – Yucky Stuff)*

With the last day of term upon us, the teacher is busy stripping walls while the class watch a DVD. We soon realise, however, that what the children think is suitable viewing material is not really what the teacher had in mind!

### *Characters*
**6 children, teacher, 7 Shakespearean characters**

### *Scene 14 – page 68*

*(associated song/s – choose from one (or all) of; Goodbye My Friend, Til The End, Wonderful Days and Every Single Step Of The Way)*

A chance for everyone to say goodbye, with a big emotional sing-song!

### *Characters*
**Your whole cast**

## *Continuity Scene*

**Note: the continuity scenes, which precede/introduce each main scene, should be considered optional, and are only suggestions of how you could link your chosen scenes together. You may prefer to omit them, or ask the children to write their own introductions, in which they reminisce or tell anecdotes about the subject matter the scene relates to.**

*(As **Intro Music** plays (CD2 - track 18) the continuity characters enter and take their positions on a smaller separate stage to one side of the main stage. This smaller stage could be made up to look like a bus stop, where Ben, Ali, Rachel and Emma, (names should be changed to those of the actors) are waiting for the school bus.)*

**Ben** ~ So, are you guys ready for your last ever day at primary school?

**Ali** ~ Well, unless this bus gets here soon it doesn't look like we're going to have a last day! We'd have been better off walking.

**Rachel** ~ It's always late on a Friday. My dad says it's something to do with Thursday night being the driver's darts night down at the pub!

**Emma** ~ I wish Sunday night was his darts night, then he'd be late on Monday morning instead.

**Ben** ~ Why? What difference does it make?

**Emma** ~ Well, think about it. If the bus is late on Monday morning, it means we'd arrive at school late on Monday morning. We'd avoid all the chaos!

**Ali** ~ Ah yes, the madness that is our Monday morning routine!

**Rachel** ~ But I love all that! The hustle and bustle, and the frantic to-ing and fro-ing! It leaves you in no doubt that another school week has well and truly begun!

## *Scene 1*

*(The action crosses to the main stage where chairs and tables are arranged, as in a classroom, for 12 children. A teacher sits nervously arranging items on his/her desk, and looking at his/her watch. S/he will have a lot of lines so these could be written on the registers s/he is holding. The children are yet to enter.)*

**Teacher** ~ Right. Ok. It's a new week, which means a fresh start and a clean slate. Last Monday morning was just a blip, a one off.....and so was the one before that..... and the one before that! I'm determined today will be different. Books are marked, the registers are ready, the morning's activities are planned...*(looking at watch and breathing deeply)*.... right....here goes....five, four, three, two, one........ *A **School Bell** is heard (CD2 - track 19)*

*(5 children - Sarah, Hannah, Peter, Becky and Lee (names should be changed to those of the children playing the characters) charge into the classroom. All but Lee sit at tables and begin to chatter. Lee stands unnoticed just behind the teacher's shoulder, patiently holding an envelope.)*

**_Teacher_** ~ Thank you Year 6. Settle down please while……..

**_Sarah_** ~ Mr/Mrs ( name ), someone's stolen my indoor shoes.

**_Teacher_** ~ They're probably in lost property along with half your other school clothes. Now Year 6, can I have some quiet for the regis…

**_Sarah_** ~ Shall I go and look.

**_Teacher_** ~ Not now, wait until I've done the regist…….

**_Peter_** ~ *(getting up and walking back out)* Silly me! I've still got my coat on.

**_Teacher_** ~ Come back and sit down. I can't have you wandering about while I'm trying to do the register. *(He sits)* Thank you. Right *(looking at register)*. Simon Atkins…… Simon Atkins? Has anyone seen Simon?

**_Peter_** ~ *(getting up and walking back out)* He's still in the cloakroom trying to untie his laces. Shall I fetch him?

**_Teacher_** ~ Oh…yes, but quickly. *(He exits)* Peter Brown…Peter Brown? Where is Peter Brown?

**_Becky_** ~ You just sent him out to fetch Simon Atkins. Shall I go and get him?

**_Teacher_** ~ No! I can't have anyone else leaving the room. *(shouting)* Simon! Peter! Hurry up! Josephine Carter…..Josephine Carter? Where is Josephine Carter.

**_Hannah_** ~ She wasn't ~~on the bus.~~ *in the playground* Her sister's in Year 3. Shall I go and ask her where she is?

**_Teacher_** ~ *(getting flustered)* No!

**_Sarah_** ~ Mr/Mrs ( name ), what about my shoes. Mum says if I lose any more…..

**_Teacher_** ~ Not now Sarah.

*(Peter comes back, now without his coat on, accompanied by Simon. They sit.)*

**_Simon & Peter_** ~ We're here!

**_Teacher_** ~ Yes, thank you. I can see that. Right, Sarah Gardner.

**_Sarah_** ~ Here!

**_Teacher_** ~ Good. Hannah Johnson.

**_Hannah_** ~ Here!

**Teacher** ~ Good. Now we're getting somewhere. Josh McKenzie…….Josh McKenzie? Has anyone seen Josh McKenzie?

**Simon** ~ He's in the loo putting on hair gel.

**Teacher** ~ Right, *(standing and shouting)* will everybody who is outside gelling their hair, putting on makeup, swapping stickers, chatting about last night's Hollyoaks or doing anything else they shouldn't be, please move your lazy behinds in here now!

*(Josh, Laura, William, Oliver and Lucy (again names should be changed to those of the children playing the characters) noisily enter and sit down.)*

Thank you. Quiet please. *(Sitting down)* Right. Who's next…Becky Parker?

**Becky** ~ Here.

**Teacher** ~ Good. Lee Pearson.

*(Lee is still standing unnoticed at the teacher's shoulder. On hearing his name he leans forward and yells…)*

**Lee** ~ Here!

*(The teacher jumps off his/her chair like a startled rabbit!)*

**Teacher** ~ Aaaah! Oh goodness me, Lee! Don't ever do that again. You nearly gave me a heart attack! Go and sit down.

**Lee** ~ But I've got my dinner money and permission slip for our trip.

**Teacher** ~ Take them back to your place. I'm collecting those when I've done this register. *(He sits)* Lucy Roberts? *(She replies)* Good. William Scott? *(He replies)* Thank you. Laura Turner? *(She replies)* And finally Oliver Watson? *(He replies)* Good. At last. OK, would anyone with dinner money please bring it to…

*(Josephine's mum appears at the door with her daughter.)*

**Mum** ~ Excuse me Mr/Mrs ( name ), I'd like a quick word about Josephine.

**Teacher** ~ Well, if you could wait five minutes, Mrs Carter, I'm just about to do the dinner regist…..

*(She barges her way to the teacher's table dragging Josephine, and proceeds to rant at the teacher, who looks gob smacked!)*

**Mum** ~ It's her chest you see. The doctor won't give her another inhaler - says her asthma has cleared up, but what does he know. He doesn't have to listen to her wheezing her way up the stairs every evening. Anyway, I'd rather she didn't do PE today. I know it's warm weather but you can't be too careful can you. She's like me you see. I always had a dodgy chest when I was young. Her sister's the same - you know, my Daisy in Year 3. I nearly kept them both off today but I'm having my roots done at 10 o'clock. I'd ask my mother to look after them, but with her hip she just can't manage at the moment. I tell you, she's been on a waiting list for 18 months. I wrote to our MP but he's useless. What do these politicians do all day? They certainly don't help the likes of my mother with her hip. I tell you, I shan't be voting for that lot again. Mind you, what's the alternative? My husband says he'd like to put the lot of them in a field and……

**Teacher** ~ Mrs Carter! I really don't have time for this now. Josephine can be excused from PE, but if you don't mind I must get on.

**Mum** ~ *(affronted)* Well, excuse me!

*(She stomps off and Josephine sits down.)*

**Teacher** ~ Right. Where was I? Yes. Would anyone who has dinner money with them please bring it to me. And as we're in a rush please could you also bring me your permission slips for next week's trip.

*(The teacher sits back down. Only Lee steps forward. He hands over his envelope and the teacher marks a different register.)*

Thank you Lee. Well? What a bout the rest of you. Oliver, where are your dinner money and slip?

**Oliver** ~ In my bag in the cloakroom. Shall I get it?

**Teacher** ~ Well it's no use in there is it. Yes, hurry up. *(He exits)* Lucy? Dinner money? Slip?

**Lucy** ~ Bag! Cloakroom! Fetch?

**Teacher** ~ Yes! Oh crikey! Look at the time! Right. Everybody who has left their dinner money and slip in their bag go and get it now. Quickly!.

*(They all exit, while Lee sits down. They then charge back and crowd round the teacher's desk.)*

**Laura** ~ All the other classes are in the hall for assembly.

**Teacher** ~ Yes, OK! I'm going as fast as I can! Form an orderly line please. *(They line up.)* OK, who's first. Josephine?

**Josephine** ~ I've not got mine.

**Teacher** ~ Well why on earth are you standing here then? Go and sit down. *(She sits).* Now, William.

*(William plonks down a large handful of coppers on the desk, and then unfolds a screwed-up scrap of paper.)*

**William** ~ That's all mum had round the house. She hasn't been to the bank yet this week. And here's my slip.

**Teacher** ~ No, no, no! I haven't got time to count all this. Oh! Just sit down. I'll have to do it later. Lucy, quick!

**Lucy** ~ I'm afraid I've only got a twenty pound note. Dad told me to make sure you gave me the right change after last week's incident. *(She hands over the money then fishes through her pockets)* Now…my slip…I know I've got it here somewhere. No…not that pocket…..hmmm…..no, not there either…….no…...

**Teacher** ~ *(about to blow)* Right! That's it. All of you just leave your money and slips on my desk and get yourselves into the hall now! Go on! Quickly!

*(The children dump their change and slips onto the desk and dash out, leaving the teacher, head in hands, to survey the carnage. S/he takes a deep breath then musters some energy.)*

OK, I've got about twenty minutes while they're in the hall to sort through this lot, then we'll be just about ready.

*(There is a knock at the door and Oliver comes back into the room)*

Yes Oliver, what is it now?

**Oliver** ~ Everyone's waiting for you, Mr/Mrs ( name ).

**Teacher** ~ *(confused)* Waiting for me? What do you mean? Oh no.....(realisation dawning)* Surely not? It's not…….

**Oliver** ~ Your turn to take assembly? I'm afraid so. I'll tell them you're on your way shall I?

*(Oliver exits and the teacher slumps forward on the desk.)*

**Teacher** ~ Oh, I give up!

*(**Intro Music** (CD2 - track 18) Fade out when children are in position to sing.)*

## Song 1 – Monday Morning Routine (CD2 - track 1, lyrics p11)

*(When the song finishes, play **Intro Music** (CD2 - track 18) during which tables and chairs are re-positioned in preparation for the next scene.)*

# *Monday Morning Routine*

1.    The school bell rings as a new day is dawning, *[day begins]*
      We're wide awake but the teacher's still yawning! *[not]* *[and are obviously]*
      She says, "Coats on pegs!" but they end up on the floor,
      School bags blocking the classroom door!
      To the untrained eye it looks a riot scene,
      But it's all part of our Monday morning routine. *[Daily]*

2.    There are mums lined up for a word – "Scuse me,
      My baby's got a cold so he can't do PE."
      One wants to talk about the price of school meals, *[music]* *[fees]*
      She looks quite annoyed but imagine how the teacher feels!
      She's building up a real head of steam,
      A common feature of our Monday morning routine. *[Daily]*

**Bridge**

      Doing the register's impossible
      'Cause only half of us are there.
      At this rate she'll end up in hospital
      Receiving psychiatric care!

3.    There's dinner money to collect, and permission slips
      For seventeen forthcoming school trips!
      So much to sort it's not surprising
      The temperature and the pressure's rising.
      Then like the Hulk she roars and turns bright green,
      But hey, what's new? It's just our Monday morning routine *[daily]*
      Monday morning routine – yeah! *[daily]*

## *Continuity Scene*

**<u>Ben</u>** ~ When you think about it, they've got such a lot to sort out even before lessons start, that it's not surprising teachers sometimes get a little bit wound up!

**<u>Ali</u>** ~ My mum says that never in a million years would she want to be a teacher!

**<u>Rachel</u>** ~ Well, imagine what it would be like if they didn't get the help they do from their teaching assistants. *and Mrs Rogers to help them*
*Mrs Pearce*
*Zanetti*

**<u>Emma</u>** ~ Yeah. And where would some of us be if we didn't have Mrs (<u>name of a TA in your school</u>) to go to for help when the teacher's busy?

**<u>Ben</u>** ~ Last week I came a right cropper in the playground. I must have ended up with half a ton of gravel in my knees. Mrs (<u>name</u>) was brilliant! She had me cleaned up in no time.
*Mrs Rogers.*

**<u>Ali</u>** ~ And some of the things they have to sort out with the infants…you know…those 'little accidents' that sometimes happen! Those ladies deserve a medal!

**<u>All</u>** ~ Yeah……….
*fade*

## *Scene 2*

*(The action again moves centre-stage, where six children sit at tables. A teacher stands before them, next to a white-board on which is written a lesson objective and a diagram of a right-angle triangle with dimensions marked on. A teaching assistant (TA), wearing an apron and rubber gloves, sits on a chair at the back.)*

**<u>Teacher</u>** ~ Please look at your photocopied sheet. Today we will be learning how to find the area of a right-angle triangle. Has everyone got a sheet?

**<u>Child 1</u>** ~ *(raising an arm)* I haven't.

**<u>TA</u>** ~ *(standing, and addressing the teacher)* Would you like me to deal with that?
*Pearce.*

**<u>Teacher</u>** ~ If you wouldn't mind, Mrs (<u>name</u>). *(A copy of the sheet is handed to the TA who exits to photocopy it.)* Now, while we're waiting for the photocopy, could anyone tell me how we find the area of a regular 4-sided shape?

**<u>Child 1</u>** ~ You count up the squares.

**<u>Teacher</u>** ~ Well, yes, (<u>name</u>). That's what you would do in year 2, but we're in year six now aren't we. *(The TA returns and hands a photocopy to child 1, then sits at the back with two children)* Thankyou, Mrs (<u>name</u>). Can anyone tell me how we do it in year 6? *(stony silence)* Come on, this isn't new. It's not as if you didn't do it to death in year 4………..think about the dimensional properties.

**<u>All Children</u>** ~ *(looking confusedly at each other and the audience)* The what!?

**_TA_** ~ *(to children 2 & 3 at the back)* Think about the length and breadth.

**_Child 2_** ~ Ooh, yes! You measure the length and breadth, then multiply them together. I remember.

**_Teacher_** ~ Well, of course you remember now you've been told. Thank you for your…err…..input Mrs (name). Actually, Mrs (name), we seem to be short of a few rulers for the practical activity.

**_TA_** ~ *(standing)* Would you like me to fetch extras?

**_Teacher_** ~ If you wouldn't mind. *(She exits.)* Now, what calculation is required to find the area of a right-angle triangle? *(All hands go up.)* Yes (name).

**_Child 3_** ~ Measure the length and the breadth and multiply them together.

**_Teacher_** ~ Ah ha! That's where you're wrong. And why are you wrong? I'll tell you. *(The TA returns and hands the rulers to the teacher, then sits down.)* Thank you, Mrs (name). As I was saying, the dimensional properties of a triangle are, of course, essentially dissimilar to those of its quadrilateral cousin. In essence, the notion of length and breadth needs refining when it comes to basic trigonometry.

**_All Children_** ~ *(looking confusedly at each other and the audience)* What!?

**_TA_** ~ *(to the children)* Why doesn't a triangle have the same sort of length and breadth as a rectangle, or square? Think about what the word 'tri' means.

**_Child 4_** ~ Ooh, I know. A triangle only has three sides, so you can't multiply it's length and breadth together to find the area. It wouldn't work.

**_Teacher_** ~ Well it's obvious when someone tells you isn't it!

**_Child 4_** ~ But she didn't………

**_Teacher_** ~ Right, moving on. Please look at the board while I demonstrate how we do, in fact, calculate the area of a right-angle triangle. First we measure the base of the triangle, then the perpendicular height to the point at which it meets the hypotenuse. By halving the base measurement and multiplying it by this perpendicular height we can generate the area. Ok, any questions?

*(All the children look bewildered!)*

**_Child 5_** ~ Could you please explain that again. What's a hi..hi..hippopotamuse?

**_Teacher_** ~ *(huffing)* Well if you paid attention first time. Oh, alright. The hypotenuse is the side opposite the angle created by the base meeting the perpendicular side. It is however redundant in the calculation of the area.

**_All Children_** ~ What!?

**_Teacher_** ~ Oh really! This is getting beyond a joke. I really........*(there is a knock at the door.)* Yes, what is it? *(Two timid infants enter, holding hands.)*

**_Infants_** ~ Could Miss (<u>name</u>) please borrow your oil pastels?

**_TA_** ~ *(standing)* Would you like me to deal with that?

**_Teacher_** ~ If you wouldn't mind, Mrs (<u>name</u>). *(The TA takes a box from the back and gently escorts the infants off stage, by the hand.)* Good, now to continue. The hypotenuse of a right-angle triangle is really the bisection of an associated quadrilateral. *(TA returns and sits.)*

**_Child 6_** ~ *(on the verge of tears)* Please. I don't know what you mean. *(The TA moves to child 6 to offer comfort.)*

**_Teacher_** ~ Look. You halve the base of the.............*(another knock at the door)* WHAT IS IT NOW!? *(Two more timid infants enter, holding hands.)*

**_Children_** ~ Can you please come and make the DVD player work in our class.

**_TA_** ~ *(standing)* Would you like me to ........

**_Teacher_** ~ No, I'll go. I'm the only one who can do it. Right, while I'm gone you can complete the area problems on your sheets. *(Exits)*

**_All Children_** ~ *(crowding round TA)* Mrs (<u>name</u>), can you help me / I don't understand / what's a hippopotamuse / what are we supposed to do etc etc.....

**_TA_** ~ OK, OK, calm down. Look, come and sit on the carpet. Let's sort it out.

*(The children sit in front of her as she stands by the white board, over which she drapes her rubber gloves.)*

Right. What's the area of this shape?

*(She draws a rectangle and writes the dimensions 10 x 8. All hands go up)*

**_All Children_** ~ Eighty!

**_TA_** ~ Excellent. Now look. I'm dividing the rectangle in half with a diagonal line. What have I made?

**_All Children_** ~ Two right-angle triangles!

*(At this point the teacher re-enters, notices what's going on, and sits gob-smacked at the back, watching.)*

**_TA_** ~ Yes! That's right. Now can you see, the area of one of the triangles is.....

**_All Children_** ~ Exactly half of the area of the rectangle!

**_TA_** ~ You've got it! Now..........*(noticing the teacher)* Oh! Sorry. They just asked if I'd..........

**_Teacher_** ~ No, no Mrs (<u>name</u>), you carry on.

**_TA_** ~ Oh. Ok. Right. So if a rectangle with a width - or base - of 8, and a length - or height - of ten, has an area of 80, then a......

**_All Children_** ~ Right-angle triangle with a base of 8 and a height of 10 must have an area of 40. Half the base times the height. Yeah!

**_TA_** ~ Excellent! Now go back to your places and try and work out the areas of the triangles on your sheet. If there are any problems just ask. *(There is another knock at the door.)* Yes, come in.

*(Two more timid infants enter, holding hands.)*

**_Infants_** ~ Sam in our class didn't make it to the toilet in time! He needs sorting!

*(The TA and teacher look at the infants, then each other.)*

**_Teacher_** ~ *(standing to address the TA)* Would you like me to deal with that?

**_TA_** ~ *(holding out the rubber gloves)* If you wouldn't mind, Mr/Mrs (<u>name</u>).

*(**Intro Music** (CD2 - track 18) Fade out when children are in position to sing.)*

## Song 2 – _Hey! T.A._ (CD2 - track 2, lyrics p16)

*(When the song finishes, play **Intro Music** (CD2 - track 18) during which tables and chairs are moved out of the way in preparation for the next scene.)*

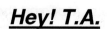

*Girl's props ready in interval.*

# Hey! T.A.

1. Who's a whizz with scissors and a staple-gun?
   Who do we turn to, to get the impossible done?
   Who can liven up the dullest wall,
   And finish in no time at all?
   Laughing off a paper-cut that would make a grown man cry….

   *Miss Zoratti (Jas)*

   Hey! T.A.
   Nowt gets in the way
   Of another great display,
   To brighten up our day.

2. Who's on hand with a bandage and sympathy,
   To remove the gravel from your knee?
   And when an infant….shall we say
   Gets caught short at morning play,
   Who's the first one on the scene with rubber gloves and bleach…

   *Mrs Rogers Marsh. (Lucy)*

   Hey! T.A.
   You're not one to delay,
   You're in there right away,
   To brighten up our day.

   *Repeat*

3. Who's got multi-tasking to a tee?
   Who can make things happen magically?
   Who can make the photo-copier do
   Everything she wants it to?
   Including A3, double-sided! How? We'll never know…

   *Mrs Pearce. Marsh. (Abi)*

   Hey! T.A.      *Repeat.*
   Your scent of PVA,
   Poster paints and clay,
   Brightens up our day.
   Hey! T.A.
   You're with me all the way,
   At work, at rest, at play,
   You brighten up my day.

   *Mrs Ansas (Sophie)*
   *Mrs Sykes (Eliane)*
   *Mrs Brook (Adi)*
   *Mrs Pring (Ella)*
   *Mrs Rimer (Leah)*

   *Mrs Sainsbury (Molly)*    *Mrs Price (Holl)*
   *Mrs Windell (Kath)*        *Mrs Channon (Le)*
   *Mrs Westmore (Emma)*    *Mrs Chapman (Gemma)*

## *Continuity Scene*

**_Emma_** ~ So, do you think we'll be doing PE today? You know, with it being our last day?

**_Ali_** ~ I hope so. I've brought my kit!

**_Rachel_** ~ Well that's a first! You normally forget it and have to cobble something together from lost property.

**_Ben_** ~ My dad says that when he was at school, if you forgot your PE kit, the teacher made you do it in pants and vest!

**_Ali_** ~ No way! They'd never do that! He's having you on!

**_Ben_** ~ Maybe, but if they did it nowadays I bet you'd soon stop forgetting your kit.

**_Emma_** ~ I don't understand why anyone would forget their kit in the first place. PE is my favourite lesson. It's the highlight of my week!

**_Rachel_** ~ Hmmm…sometimes I like it, sometimes I don't. I think it all depends on who's teaching it………….

## *Scene 3*

*(The action again moves centre stage where a stern, tracksuited teacher, with a rake and a clip board, marches on like a drill sergeant, faces the audience, flexes, then blows a whistle. If there is a teacher at your school who is very keen on competitive sport, organising teams etc, and can take a joke, you could liken this character to them, with regard to clothes, hair and name etc. This character will have a lot to say so lines can be referred to/read from the clip board.)*

**_Teacher_** ~ MOVE YOURSELVES! MOVE YOURSELVES! HUP HUP HUP!

*(A selection of children, in a variety of 'kit', run on and sit at the front of the stage facing back towards the teacher. One child with a bandaged knee hobbles on behind the rest and sits down with real effort.)*

**_Teacher_** ~ *(menacingly)* Ok you feeble lot, I'm going to get you long-jumping properly if it's the last thing I do. Look at the state of you two. Stand up! You call that 'kit'?

*(A boy wearing baggy 'skater' shorts and a top with the hood up, and a girl wearing jewellery, heels and mini-skirt, both stand up.)*

**_Girl_** ~ *(folds arms with attitude)* I thought it was going to rain all day today, right, so I naturally assumed we'd be doing PE inside.

**_Teacher_** ~ *(sarcastically)* Of course, what you're wearing is perfect for indoor PE, isn't it. Heels and a mini-skirt! Twice round the field. GO! *(She clip-clops off)* And you're not going to break any records wearing that. What's your excuse?

**_Boy_** ~ *(inaudible grunt)*

**_Teacher_** ~ I'm sorry, I didn't catch that.

**_Boy_** ~ *(a louder and longer inaudible grunt)*

**_Teacher_** ~ Of course, how silly of me. I should have guessed. Twice round the field. GO! *(The boy slouches off)* Right, everybody. Make an orderly line over there and let's get ready for some long jump.

*(The remaining children line up in front of the stage, to one side. Each child takes it in turn to run along the front of the stage, and jump as if into a pit. The teacher watches from the stage.)*

Right, first one. Let's go!

*(The first child makes a half-hearted effort)*

What was that? No, no. You need to stamp off the board when you've reached your maximum speed. Throw your arms and legs forward and don't sit back in the sand. 1 metre 20. NEXT!

*(The next child jumps)*

No jump! Your foot was way over the board. Did you measure your run up? How many times have I told you to measure your run up? Does nobody listen to me? NEXT!

*(The next child jumps)*

1 metre 80! What was that? Stretch! NEXT!

*(The next child jumps)*

Oh come on. A bit of effort please. I know you can jump further than that. I've seen you leaping the ditch into the out-of-bounds section of the field, when you've been playing kiss-chase! 2 metres10. NEXT!

*(The next child jumps)*

Long jump! It's called long jump! We therefore require a little bit of length! Do you understand? 1 metre 60. NEXT!

*(The child with the bandaged leg hobbles painfully along the front of the stage)*

Oh come on! Your knee operation was two weeks ago for goodness' sake. Honestly! Do none of you lot care that I've got an athletics team to pick for the area championships, where it looks like we're going to be a laughing stock! *(looking at watch)* Right, Mrs ( name ) needs the sand pit for her class's long jump lesson, so all of you, twice round the field. GO!

*(As they march out they pass another teacher, dressed in a summery outfit and awkwardly carrying a rake, a magazine and a deck chair, which she unfolds and sits on, facing the audience. She puts on a pair of sunglasses and starts applying sun cream. Again, if there is a teacher at your school who is, shall we say, a little averse to the teaching of games, and who can take a joke, this character can be based on them! She will also have a lot to say, so lines can be concealed in the magazine)*

**Teacher** ~ Lovely! Ok children, gather round and listen.

*(A similar sized group as the first, similarly dressed, enters and sits by her feet.)*

**Teacher** ~ Lovely! Right. This afternoon we'll be doing some long jumping into our lovely sandpit. Now it's a warm day so I don't want you overdoing things. Just take things gently then nobody will get hot and flustered. Lovely. Ok, off you go up there and do your jumps.

*(While the children line up as before the teacher opens her magazine and starts reading. She casually glances as they jump but is more interested in the article.)*

Ok, who's first?
>    *(The first child makes a half-hearted effort)*

Oh, what a lovely jump. And look, you got into the pit. Lovely! NEXT!

>    *(The next child makes a respectable effort)*

Lovely! Didn't you go a long way. *(She continues reading)*

**Child** ~ *(disappointedly)* But it was a no jump. You didn't give me time to measure out my run-up.

**Teacher** ~ *(still reading)* Mmm? What? Yes, a lovely no-jump. Well done. NEXT!

>    *(The next child jumps as the teacher carries on reading)*

Lovely!

**Child** ~ *(excitedly)* How far was it? I think that was my best jump ever.

**Teacher** ~ *(still reading)* Mmm? What was that, Dear?

**Child** ~ I said how far was it?

**Teacher** ~ How far was what, Dear?

**Child** ~ My jump!

**Teacher** ~ Your jump? Ooh yes! Your jump! Yes, it was very, very far. Well done. Lovely! NEXT!

*(As the next girl starts her run-up the teacher stands up and excitedly stops her in her tracks.)*

Now that's a lovely skirt you're wearing! And doesn't it go well with those heels. Where did you get them?

**Girl** ~ Top Shop.

**Teacher** ~ Top Shop! Aah! They've got some lovely things in there. I'll tell you what, it would be a shame to get sand all over them, so you stand by the pit with the rake and look pretty. Lovely! NEXT!

*(The next child jumps as the teacher carries on reading)*

Lovely! NEXT!

*(As the next child jumps he/she falls forward, then pulls a face, having got a mouthful of sand.)*

**Child** ~ *(spitting)* Eurgh!

**Teacher** ~ *(startled)* My goodness! Are you alright? Have you broken anything?

**Child** ~ No, I'm fine. I just swallowed a bit of sand.

**Teacher** ~ Well, you know sand can be very dangerous to young bodies. *(to girl with rake)* Take poor ( name ) to the staffroom will you, and ask one of the ladies to look at him/her.

*(The two children exit, with protests from the sand-swallower and to looks of disbelief from the other children.)*

Right children, gather round. ( name ) has had a terrible accident, which means we have to cut short our long-jumping session. Please go back to the classroom and get changed. I'll just clear up here and I'll be along shortly. Off you go.

*(The children exit, a little bewildered. The teacher watches that they've all gone, then sits back down and picks up the magazine.)*

Right…Sagittarius….*(reading)* 'Saturn is in your house which means you really should be taking things easy'. Well, fancy that! *(contented sigh)*

*(**Intro Music** (CD2 - track 18) Fade out when children are in position to sing.)*

## Song 3 – PE Nightmare (CD2 - track 3, lyrics p21)

*(When the song finishes, play **Intro Music** (CD2 - track 18) during which chairs are re-positioned in preparation for the next scene.)*

# *PE Nightmare*

1. The weather is what you'd call 'inclement',
   Cold and blustery.
   Half the day is done but the worst is yet to come
   'Cause we've still got to do PE.
   It's like there's a time-bomb ticking
   As we await the call…
   "Books away! Get changed! Quick march! Line up
   Outside against the wall!"

2. We're waiting for the stragglers
   Who say they've lost their kit.
   We shiver and we shake, we quiver and we quake
   'Cause the wind's picked up a bit.
   As we turn blue, our teacher
   Finds it so hard not to gloat,
   'Cause we're in flimsy vests and shorts
   And she's in her winter coat!

3. First it's twice around the field,
   A 'warm-up' as it's known.
   That's such a stupid phrase, and it's really not the case
   'Cause we're frozen to the bone!
   Jumping over puddles,
   And the spots where dogs have 'been',
   Trying, without much success,
   To keep our trainers clean.

4. The torture is finally over,
   At least until next week,
   When I think I'll bring a note, which I'll say the doctor wrote,
   About me having flat feet!
   But then a spanner's thrown
   Into this cunning little scheme…..
   The teacher's made me captain
   Of the school cross-country team!

## Continuity Scene

**_Emma_** ~ This ridiculous. The bus should have been here ten minutes ago.

**_Ali_** ~ And by the time it does get here the driver will be in really bad mood.

**_Rachel_** ~ Yeah, just like that one who took us on our last school trip. Do you remember, that 'really great' visit to the zoo? Not!

**_Ben_** ~ Oh, I don't know. That trip had its moments!

**_Ali_** ~ You're kidding! It was a complete wash-out! Surely you remember…..

## Scene 4

*(The action moves to the front of centre stage where a teacher in a bobble hat, waterproof coat, hiking boots, carrying a ruck-sack and holding a clipboard and compass, is addressing a class of children with bags, who are standing in a group on the floor in front of the stage. Two other adult helpers are standing nervously to the side. One is holding a medical bag. Along the back wall of the stage is an arrangement of chairs to represent a bus.)*

**_Teacher_** ~ *(to the helpers)* Mrs (<u>name</u>), Mrs (<u>name</u>), would you just do a quick head-count for me while I check the itinerary.

*(The two anxiously try to count but the children are moving around.)*

**_Helper 1_** ~ I make it thirteen. You?

**_Helper 2_** ~ Erm, seventeen! Oh dear! *(They attempt a second count.)*

**_Helper 2_** ~ Nine?

**_Helper 1_** ~ Twenty four! Oh dear!

**_Teacher_** ~ *(noticing their inept effort)* Oh, for goodness sake. Children. Stand still. *(They continue moving)* CHILDREN! PLEASE STAND STILL! Thank you. Now…*(counting heads)*…Good. All present and correct. OK. We have a marvellous trip planned. It's a special day at the zoo today. Apparently Chi Chi the panda is expected to give birth. It is a very rare occasion and we are going to be lucky enough to witness it.

**_Child 1_** ~ Will we be allowed on the arcade machines? Mum gave me £10 and she didn't mention anything about bringing change back. *(The teacher sighs.)*

**_Child 2_** ~ I heard they've got a wicked ride there. Will we get time to go on it?

**_Teacher_** ~ Honestly! We'll be present at an historic and beautiful event, the birth of a baby panda, and all you can think about is slot machines and rollercoasters!

**_Child 3_** ~ Will there be a telly on the bus? Can we watch it?

**_Teacher_** ~ What? No! Please try to get into the spirit of things. This trip has taken a lot of organising and we won't be wasting time on things like TV. Now the bus is here. A quick head-count please, ladies.

*(Another futile attempt to count is made as the children continually move. A bus driver enters and sits at the front of the arrangement of chairs)*

**_Helper 1_** ~ I make it sixteen. You?

**_Helper 2_** ~ Twenty one! Oh dear!

**_Teacher_** ~ *(losing patience)* CHILDREN! PLEASE STAND STILL!...*(counting)*... Thank you. Now, without any fuss, please take your seats on the bus.

*(In a scramble, all the children end up crammed on the back seats.)*

Ladies, would you sort out the seating, while I talk to the driver. Oh, and could you do another head-count. Thanks.

**_Helper 1 & 2_** ~ Oh dear! *(Nothing is accomplished, as noticed by the driver.)*

**_Driver_** ~ *(adopting a menacing stance)* OI! ANY NONSENSE AND YER OFF! NOW MOVE YERSELVES!

*(The children quickly move to fill the empty seats, leaving some 'larger' boys smiling at the back. The adults sit at the front.)*

**_Boys_** ~ *(chanting)* BACK SEAT! BACK SEAT! WE'RE THE BACK SEAT BOYS!

**_Child 4_** ~ *(shouting down the bus to the adults)* Can we open our pack lunches? I'm starving. I didn't have any breakfast.

**_Helper 1_** ~ *(turning in her seat and shouting back)* Now that's not such a good idea, is it. You'll just eat sweets, and we all know what that can lead to.

**_Child 5_** ~ Can we play with our Nintendos?

**_Helper 2_** ~ Wouldn't it be better to look out the window and enjoy the scenery. You know, it might stop the old..err..tummy upset. Ooh, which reminds me. *(She approaches the teacher and whispers something.)*

**_Teacher_** ~ Oh yes. Mrs (name) has reminded me to ask those of you who get travel sick to sit at the front on newspaper.

*(Several sheets are removed from the ruck-sack and placed on seats near the front behind the adults, after the occupants are asked to stand. Three children are moved from the back seat to swap with children nearer the front.)*

**_Child 6_** ~ What a load of old cobblers! How on earth can sitting on newspaper stop you feeling travel-sick. They must think we were born yesterday.

**_Child 7_** ~ Yeah, my auntie's a doctor and she says there's nothing newspaper can do except leave print on your bottom, which is murder to get clean.

**_Driver_** ~ Are we ready then, or what? I have got other jobs on today y'know. I mean, I can't be 'anging around 'ere waiting for this rabble to sort themselves.

**_Teacher_** ~ I think we are. OK, off we go!

*(The **bus revs up** (CD2 - track 20) then lurches off – shown by a uniform leaning-back of the passengers and driver. The adults, who are standing at the time stumble to their seats. The children, simultaneously and together, take a lunch box from their bag, remove the lid, open a pack of sweets, stuff a handful in their mouths, take out a games console, lower their heads and begin playing. The teacher and helpers sit singing 'The wheels on the bus' until, from the back...)*

**_Child 8_** ~ Eugh! No! (name) has been sick. It's everywhere!

*(All the children hold their noses and pull faces. The driver looks annoyed.)*

**_Driver_** ~ Now look 'ere. I'm tellin' yer now, I am not clearin' that up. Why should I clear that up? It's not my job to clean up after little tykes who don't know how to feed themselves. I never wanted to take this job. School trips are nothing but...

**_Teacher_** ~ Oh, be quiet! *(calling down the bus)* (name), come and sit down here. We'll clean you up when we get there. It's not far now.

**_Helper 1 & 2_** ~ *(smugly, to children sitting near them)* You see. That's what happens when you don't sit on newspaper.

*(A child vacates one of the front seats and a helper covers it with newspaper. The sick child sits and the journey continues with everyone holding their noses, including the driver. After a moment the **bus stops** (CD2 - track 21) this time shown by a uniform leaning-forward of the passengers and driver.)*

**_Teacher_** ~ Ok everybody, we've arrived. Could you all get off the bus sensibly and quietly while I check our tickets. Mrs (name), Mrs (name), would you just do another quick head-count for me.

*(The helpers try to count as the children noisily stand down from the stage.)*

**_Helper 1_** ~ I make it twenty-seven. You?

**_Helper 2_** ~ Errm, thirty-three! Oh dear!

**_Teacher_** ~ Oh, for goodness sake. CHILDREN! PLEASE STAND STILL! ... *(counting)*...Thank you. Now, walk in twos and follow me.

**_Announcement 1_** ~ *(either read out from backstage or use **CD2 - track 22**)* Ladies and gentlemen, boys and girls. We have been informed by the keepers at the panda enclosure that Chi Chi is about to give birth. If you don't want to miss this historic event we suggest you make your way there immediately.

**_Teacher_** ~ Ooh, quickly! Follow me.

*(The disorganised group moves around the room ushered by the teacher and helpers. We hear the announcer's voice again, read out or **CD2 - track 23**)*

**_Announcement 2_** ~ This is the final call for anyone wishing to witness the historic birth of Chi Chi's baby. Please come to the panda enclosure. We are moments away.

**_Teacher_** ~ Quick, quick. Come on. Nearly there....Oh do hurry up. This is a once-in-a-lifetime chance which I don't intend missing....OK, here we are.

*(The teacher and helpers stand on stage, facing the audience, with the children in front of them, facing the stage, straining to look over the adult's shoulders.)*

Ok, just before we go in, another head–count please ladies.

**_Helper 1_** ~ I make it fifteen. You?

**_Helper 2_** ~ Errm, forty-eight! Oh dear!

**_Teacher_** ~ Oh, for goodness' sake! CHILDREN! PLEASE STAND STILL!...The sooner we get this done, the sooner we see the birth.

*(As the teacher is mouthing numbers, we hear a cheer from a crowd and the announcer's voice – **CD2 - track 24**) At this the school party freezes.)*

**_Announcement 3_** ~ And there we have it ladies and gentleman, boys and girls. A once-in-a-lifetime, never-to-be-missed opportunity. It's a beautiful baby for Chi Chi. What a spectacle! What a day! Now ladies and gentlemen, boys and girls, out of respect for the special couple, we ask that you leave the panda enclosure calmly and quietly. Thank you everyone, and goodbye.

*(The children turn to the audience in disbelief, while the adults look sheepish.)*

**_Children_** ~ *(sarcastically and exasperated)* Oh brilliant!

*(**Intro Music** (CD2 - track 18) Fade out when children are in position to sing.)*

## Song 4 – _School Trip Boogie_ (CD2 - track 4, lyrics p26)

*(When the song finishes, play **Intro Music** (CD2 - track 18) during which chairs and tables are re-positioned in preparation for the next scene.)*

## *School Trip Boogie*

1. Well Mum's packed the sandwiches
   And wrapped us up in winter-wear.
   She thinks we'll catch a chill
   But it's 26 degrees out there.
   And as she waves goodbye,
   There's a tear in her eye,
   But we're far too busy on the back seat to even care!

2. There's a headless chicken
   We assume is running the show,
   With a teaching assistant
   And a first-aid bag in tow.
   She counted our heads and then
   Did it five more times again!
   Totally regretting that she ever volunteered to go.

3. So sitting on a newspaper
   Stops you feeling sick on the way?
   And looking out the window
   Keeps the nausea at bay?
   But when you've eaten several packs
   Of sweet and sickly snacks,
   You'll be heaving in a lay-by on the dual carriageway!

4. Now we're back, and our teacher
   Seems relatively calm.
   And vomiting aside
   There's been no real cause for alarm.
   But when it's over and done
   The worst is yet to come……..
   Next term's trip has already been planned
   And nobody's offering to give her a hand.
   Well, who wants to spend a day at the sewage farm?

## *Continuity Scene*

**_Rachel_** ~ I'll tell you, there's one thing I'm certainly not going to miss when we've left primary school…..tests.

**_Ben_** ~ What are you talking about? We'll have ten times as many tests when we get to the next place, and not just in English, Maths and Science.

**_Rachel_** ~ What?!

**_Ali_** ~ He's right. It's not just SATs they do. There are exams and tests in every subject. Then we'll do these things called GCSEs that are dead difficult and dead important!

**_Emma_** ~ They'll make the tests we did here seem like such a breeze, even though at the time we thought we couldn't work any harder.

**_Rachel_** ~ Well at least we've got the summer holidays to look forward to, before we need to worry about any more stupid SATs or exams. Eurgh! The thought of them still brings me out in a cold sweat…………

## *Scene 5*

*(The action again moves centre stage, to where three tables are arranged as in previous scenes. One chair is behind each table. Facedown on each table is a science SAT paper. Three children enter. The first two look nervous and carry a pencil case and a selection of stuffed toys/teddies/mascots etc. The third casually saunters on with a pencil in his/her mouth. They sit down and the nervous two arrange their mascots, while the third yawns and leans back on the chair.* **Suggestion – the words that follow for each child are the thoughts they are having as the test proceeds. It would be very effective for the children to record this dialogue as it is written, the whole of which can be played over your loud speakers. Each child's actions and facial expressions, when accompanying their recorded voices, will show their feelings towards the situation they are in. If this is not possible perhaps three other children could read backstage into a microphone. Alternatively the three actors could speak the words as 'asides'.)**

**_Teacher_** ~ *(voice heard from off-stage)* Right, you have thirty-five minutes. You may turn your papers over now.

**_Child 1_** ~ *(clasping hand to mouth on turning over the paper)* Science! Not Science! I thought it was English this morning! Oh no! I can't remember a thing. *(breathing deeply)* It's ok. Just relax. Concentrate. *(S/he begins reading.)*

**_Child 2_** ~ *(anxiously)* Right, I've got to try and look at the notes written on the paper tucked up my sleeve without the teacher spotting me. Good, s/he's turned around. *(rummaging up sleeve)* Got it. Right…..What! Oh no s/he's coming over! Someone ask for a spare pencil or something….Phew! S/he's been distracted by Anna discussing her answers with Katherine.

**_Child 3_** ~ *(casually looking at the cover)* So what do we have here then? Surname? Yes, I know that one. *(writes)* First name? Yes, I know that one too! *(writes)* And School? These questions are so easy! *(writes)* Well that's 100% so far. Let's see what's next. *(turning page and reading on)*

**_Child 1_** ~ *(reading)* 'How does a plant pho..to..syn..the..sise?' What on earth does that mean? We haven't done that this year. I know what the roots of a plant are for, *(flicking through the pages)* but there aren't any questions about that as far as I can see! Oh no!

**_Child 2_** ~ *(gesturing wildly)* Got to catch Emily's eye. Oh Emily, please look this way. Please! She'll know the answer to number five. Go on, stand your paper up…move your arm….turn the page slowly! Anything so I can see what you've written. Please, just look this…….*(freezes with arms in air)* Oh no, teacher's seen me waving! *(Yawning)* Just having a stretch, nothing to see here!

**_Child 3_**~ *(reading)* 'Name the process in which water turns into water vapour'. Now, if I time this just right *(taking a chewed up piece of paper from mouth and attaching it to the end of a ruler)* I can get Simon on the back of the neck with this spit-ball. *(fires it)* Oops! I hit Mrs/Miss/Mr (_name_). Quick, innocent expression. La la la la…..

**_Child 1_** ~ *(grumpily looking around)* Look at them all, scribbling away. Swots! I hate them. They think they're so clever. *(sighing)* I might as well straighten my teddies…..sharpen my pencil……straighten my teddies….Oh look at them all. I hate them!

**_Child 2_** ~ Right, I know. I'll ask to go to the toilet, get my notes out of my bag, pretend I've got a bad case of the runs, and sit on the loo for five minutes revising! Yes, five minutes should do it. *(puts hand up)*

**_Teacher_** ~ *(voice heard from off-stage)* Right, you have five minutes left.

**_Child 2_** ~ What!

**_Child 3_** ~ *(reading)* Can you name the major organs of a flowering plant?' Errm…*(considers answer, then writes)* Yes.. I.. can…full stop. *(smiling)* Good. Ok, on to the next question.

**_Child 1_** ~ *(reading)* 'How long does it take the earth to orbit the sun once?' But I thought the sun orbited the earth! Oh no! *(frantically turning pages)* There's got to be one question in here that I know the answer to. There's just got to be.

**_Child 2_** ~ *(desperately constructing something)* Ok, so we've all been given a mirror to help with the question on reflection and light. If I attach my mirror to the end of a ruler with the chewing gum that's stuck under the table, I'll be able to hold it up and look behind me at Daniel's paper and see what he's written. Here goes. *(holding up the device)* Oh no! Just my luck to be sitting in front of the boy with the worst handwriting in the world! *(folds arms and sulks)* And now I'm right out of cheating ideas.

**_Child 3_** ~ The cover of this SAT paper is just the right size to make an excellent paper aeroplane. *(rips it off)* Let's see, open it out…..fold the corners to the middle…..and once more…..fold in half…..fold the edges down…..a nip here…a tuck there……and …..perfect! Now, let's see how this baby flies. *(throws it)* Wow!

**_Child 1_** ~ *(jumping up excitedly)* Yes! Yes! I've found one I can do! *(reading)* 'Put these living organisms into a food chain in the correct order; lettuce, cat, thrush, slug.' Yes, I know it! *(thinking it through)* Lettuce is eaten by slug, so that's an arrow from lettuce to slug. Slug is eaten by thrush, so that's an arrow from slug to thrush. And thrush is eaten by cat, so that's an arrow from thrush to cat. And it's for four marks. Right….. *(lifts pencil to write)*

**_Teacher_** ~ *(voice heard from off-stage)* Time's up everyone. Please put your pens and pencils down now.

**_Child 1_** ~ *(out loud)* WHAT!

**_Child 2_** ~ *(out loud)* YOU'RE KIDDING!

**_Child 3_** ~ *(out loud as he dashes off)* Cool! Playtime. I'm outa here!

*(**Intro Music** (CD2 - track 18) Fade out when children are in position to sing.)*

## Song 5 – _The SATs Blues_ (CD2 - track 5, lyrics p30)

*(When the song finishes, play **Intro Music** (CD2 - track 18) during which chairs are moved re-positioned in preparation for the next scene.)*

# The SATs Blues

1.    I woke up this morning in the grip of fear!
     The thing that I've been dreading most is finally here!
     I could try and throw a 'sicky'
     Or come up with another excuse,
     But there's no getting over it
     I've got a bad case of SATs blues!

2.    I stare at the paper, it's staring at me.
     I forgot the facts about electricity!
     Evaporation? Condensation?
     Need some inspiration or clues!
     'Cause there's no getting over it
     I've got a bad case of SATs blues!

3.    The clock's a-ticking, not even halfway through!
     I forgot my five times table – it's the only one I knew!
     Multiply or take away?
     Divide? I don't know which one to use.
     Well there's no getting over it
     I've got a bad case of SATs blues!

*Projector*

4.    Got spelling amnesia creeping up on me!
     Is it T..H..E..I..R or T..H..E..R..E?
     Is it 'HEAR' or 'HERE', 'WHERE' or 'WEAR'
     'WITCH' or 'WHICH' one should I choose?
     Oh there's no getting over it
     I've got a bad case of SATs blues!

*Projector*

## *Continuity Scene*

**_Ben_** ~ Do you know what's really annoying about this bus being late? I could have had an extra bowl of cereal and two more slices of toast, instead of rushing to get here!

**_Ali_** ~ Well, I always make sure I've had plenty of breakfast, just in case I don't like what they've cooked for school lunch.

**_Rachel_** ~ What do you mean? School lunches have never been better. Every cook's so worried that Jamie Oliver's going to turn up and tell them how they're poisoning us, that they're all making a real effort.

**_Emma_** ~ You have to admit, the food is really good. It's just all the other stuff that goes on now which is a real drag.

**_Ben_** ~ Like what? I have packed lunches so I don't really know what's changed with school dinners.

**_Emma_** ~ Well, let me explain..........

## *Scene 6*

*(The action again crosses to the main stage where 4 tables are elaborately set for dinner, with a table cloth, linen napkins, a candle, 2 wine glasses, an ice bucket, a single rose in a small vase and fancy cutlery for starters, mains and desserts. Each table is set for two. Four cooks in white aprons sit at two of the tables, exhausted. They have a copy of Jamie Oliver's 'School Dinners' book.)*

**_Cook 1_** ~ I don't think I can do this for much longer. *(waving the book)* I'm working an eighteen hour day just to keep up with this lot.

**_Cook 2_** ~ I was in at 6.30am today to get those duck breasts marinating, and to be here for that delivery of asparagus. I'm exhausted!

**_Cook 3_** ~ Well I've been chopping shallots and garlic since daybreak! I absolutely stink!

**_Cook 4_** ~ That's nothing. I was down at the docks at 4 o'clock this morning queuing up for fresh shellfish. That Pierre from the French restaurant said I jumped the queue and we nearly got into a punch-up. He was just jealous 'cause I bagged the best lobsters. Not a good start to my day.

**_Cook 1_** ~ Well I just hope these kids appreciate what we're doing for them. I mean, I really don't know what was wrong with what we cooked before all these changes. It was tasty and filling, which is all they cared about.

**_Cook 2_** ~ But now we can't serve burgers. No, it has to be medium rare fillet of Aberdeen Angus. And what was so wrong with fish fingers? Now it's sea bass steamed with spring onions and ginger!

**_Cook 3_** ~ And we always served veg. We'd open a can of mixed carrots, peas and sweet corn and they'd be happy. But oh no, that's not good enough for the little darlings. Now its gratinated spinach, porcini mushrooms and mange tout!

**_Cook 4_** ~ And puddings! I used to whip up a great treacle sponge and custard – OK, it was from a packet, but it tasted great. Now It's.....what is it.....pass the book... *(putting on specs and reading)* 'Pears poached in cassis with vanilla mascarpone'. It's ridiculous.

**_Cook 1_** ~ Crikey! Look at the time! They'll be in any minute. Quick! Back to the kitchen. Come on, hurry!

*(They rush off. Five dinner ladies enter, dressed in tabards. Four stand by a table each, whilst the fifth 'floats' between tables with an authoritative air.)*

**_Dinner Lady 5_** ~ *(with a French accent if possible)* OK ladies, I shall be working front of house today. I expect efficient yet friendly service from all of you. Don't let me down. Mrs ( name ), if you would be so kind.

*(Dinner Lady 2 produces a gong and hits it.)*

**_Dinner Lady 2_** ~ Dinner is served.

*(Looking very uncomfortable, four boys dressed in dinner suits each escort a girl in a gown to a table. **The following eleven actions should be synchronised so each table performs the same movements at the same time**. 1.Each of the four dinner ladies by a table pulls the chair out for the girl who sits. 2.The same is then done for the boy. 3.They then unfold the napkins and place them on the girls' then boys' laps. 4.They hand the girl then boy a menu, and ask....)*

**_Dinner Ladies 1, 2, 3 & 4_** ~ Would Monsieur like to see the wine list?

**_Boys 1, 2, 3 & 4_** ~ Errm...yeah....go on then.

*(5.The wine lists are presented to the boys who confusedly point to the name of a random bottle. 6.The four ladies go off in unison and each return with a bottle. 7.They pour a small amount in the boys' glasses. 8.This is nervously tasted then approved with a nod to the lady. 9.The girls', then the boys' glasses are filled. 10.The bottles are put in the ice buckets. 11.The ladies pull out a pen and pad.)*

**_Dinner Ladies 1, 2, 3 & 4_** ~ May I take your order?

*(Note: As the following interaction takes place between Dinner Lady 1 and Boy & Girl 1, the same interaction should be mimed between Dinner Lady 2 and Boy & Girl 2, and Dinner Lady 3 and Boy & Girl 3 at the same time. This will save time and repetition. If you want to extend the scene however, each order for each table can be scripted and acted out in turn. Boy 4 takes longer to read the menu, while Girl 4 seems totally disinterested. They therefore don't mime the same interaction as the other couples.)*

**_Girl 1_** ~ *(struggling to read the menu)* Errm....could I please have the...loin of pork with the....shiitake *(she pronounces it 'shee-ee-take')* mushrooms and the.... pommes dauphinoise *(she pronounces it 'pommees dorp-hin-oys')*.

**_Dinner Lady 1_** ~ Certainly Mademoiselle, the pork with shiitake mushrooms and pommes dauphinoise *(pronounced correctly)*. And for Monsieur?

**_Boy 1_** ~ *(also struggling to read the menu)* Errm…I'll have the same.

**_Dinner Lady 1_** ~ Certainly Monsieur. Would you like starters?

**_Boy 1_** ~ No thank you, we don't have time. Lessons start again in twenty-five minutes.

**_Dinner Lady 1_** ~ That's fine Monsieur, Mademoiselle. I'll be back shortly.

*(Dinner ladies 1, 2 and 3 take the menus and exit together, leaving the three couples looking nervously at each other.)*

**_Dinner Lady 4_** ~ *(to Boy 4)* Have you decided Monsieur?

**_Boy 4_** ~ *(also struggling to read the menu)* I think so. Errm…could I please have the Boeuf Bourguignon *(he pronounces it boof borg-wig-non)*

**_Dinner Lady 4_** ~ Certainly Monsieur, the Boeuf Bourguignon *(pronounced correctly)*. And for Mademoiselle?

**_Girl 4_** ~ *(producing a tupperware box)* Nothing for me thank you. I'm on packed lunches. I've brought sandwiches.

*(Dinner Lady 5 hears this and moves to their table, looking sternly at the girl.)*

**_Dinner Lady 5_** ~ *(to Dinner Lady 4)* Merci, Madame (_name_), I shall deal with this. *(To Girl 4)* I am sorry Mademoiselle, but only food purchased on the premises may be consumed on the premises. This is a high class establishment. We do not allow home-made sandwiches here! I must ask you to leave immediately.

**_Girl 4_** ~ But…..

**_Dinner Lady 5_** ~ Immediately, Mademoiselle!

*(She gestures to Dinner Lady 4 who 'escorts' the girl away, leaving the boy looking lost. All four dinner ladies then return with plates of food which they place before the waiting boys and girls. They then stand back from the tables. Boy 1 starts eating.)*

**_Dinner Lady 5_** ~ Ahem! Excusé moi. Haven't we forgotten something?

*(Everyone bows their head)*

**_All_** ~ For every cup and plateful, Lord make us truly grateful. Amen.

**_Dinner Lady 5_** ~ Thank you. Bon appetite.

*(The children cautiously begin tasting while the ladies stand back from their respective tables. Boy 2 takes his napkin off his knee and puts it in his collar. Girl 3 picks up her different sets of cutlery in turn, confused as to which one to use. Dinner Lady 5 gestures to Dinner Lady 2 that she should deal with Boy 2.)*

**Dinner Lady 2** ~ *(leaning forward)* Ahem, Monsieur. In this establishment we frown upon the wearing of one's napkin in one's collar. It is considered common. Please place it back on your knee.

**Boy 2** ~ *(looking put out)* But I do it at home, and at Burger King.

**Dinner Lady 2** ~ *(laughing patronisingly)* With respect, Monsieur, this is hardly Burger King.

*(She removes the napkin from the boy's collar and returns it to his knee. Meanwhile Girl 3 has decided which cutlery to use and begins eating. Dinner Lady 5 gasps in horror at her choice and gestures to Dinner Lady 3 to deal with her. Dinner Lady 3 leans forward and takes the knife and fork out of the girl's hand and replaces them with the correct set.)*

**Dinner Lady 3** ~ Ahem, I think Mademoiselle will find that it is this set that you should use for your main course.

**Girl 3** ~ But what does it matter which………

**Dinner Lady 3** ~ *(threateningly)* Believe me, Mademoiselle, it matters very much. We have standards these days – standards which must be upheld.

*(The girl cowers and continues eating. Boy 3 puts his hand up and Dinner Lady 3 attends to him.)*

**Boy 3** ~ I'm sorry to bother you, but my steak is really rare. I can't eat steak unless it's very well cooked. Could I possibly have another one instead?

*(All the dinner ladies gasp.)*

**Dinner Lady 5** ~ *(rushing over)* I beg your pardon!

**Boy 3** ~ What? What did I say?

**Dinner Lady 5** ~ You philistine! Well cooked steak! Chef would never hear of it. It is practically against the law these days. A steak must ooze juices and blood, and to ask for it cooked any other way is an insult to this establishment and all who work in it. So no, Monsieur, you may not have another one instead.

*(The boy, close to tears, tries to force down a mouthful but has to admit defeat. He puts his cutlery down and sips his wine. Girl 2 raises her hand, and Dinner Lady 2 attends.)*

**Girl 2** ~ Would it be possible to have some tomato ketchup please?

**_All Dinner Ladies_** ~ WHAT!?

*(The cooks rush back in looking appalled.)*

**_All Cooks_** ~ WHAT!?

*(All the children wince as Dinner Lady 5 and Cook 1 approach the girl.)*

**_Cook 1_** ~ Ketchup! You dare to ask for ketchup? We have to slave away day after day to provide you lot with the best gourmet experience you could ever possibly have. *(waving the book)* We're told to create delicate balances of flavour using the freshest ingredients we can lay our hands on. We spend our valuable time painstakingly and lovingly dressing each plate so your food looks exquisite…..and you ask for ketchup?

**_Dinner Lady 5_** ~ We try to turn you burger-munching, fast food junkies into sophisticated and cultured diners. We try to instruct you in a bit of etiquette, all because we've been told to improve standards. And what do you do? You put napkins down your collars, you use the wrong cutlery, you bring your own sandwiches and you can't pronounce anything on the menu properly. It's disgraceful. In fact you can all leave. Come on, all of you out now. Come on, leave please.

**_Boy 1_** ~ But what about pudding?

**_All Cooks and Dinner ladies_** ~ OUT!

*(The shocked children are ushered out by dinner lady 5. The remaining dinner ladies and the cooks watch them leave with disapproval. They then look at the vacant tables.)*

**_Cook 2_** ~ What about all this food?

*(Each cook and dinner lady sits down on a chair.)*

**_All_** ~ Waste not want not! Cheers!

*(They chink glasses)*

**_Dinner Lady 5_** ~ *(no longer in a French accent, to Dinner Lady 4)* Hey ( name ), be a love. Go and fetch us the ketchup.

*(**Intro Music** (CD2 - track 18) Fade out when children are in position to sing.)*

# Song 6 – _New School Dinner_ (CD2 - track 6, lyrics p36)

*(When the song finishes, play **Intro Music** (CD2 - track 18) during which chairs and tables are re-positioned in preparation for the next scene.)*

Grandpa & Dad

## *New School Dinner*

"School dinners, school dinners,
Concrete chips, concrete chips,
Sloppy semolina, sloppy semolina,
I feel sick! Fetch a bucket quick!"

1. Well that's a song that they used to sing,
But Jamie Oliver's gone and changed everything.
Now there's no single chip or burger in sight,
'Cause we don't do fat or sugar,
Or anything that's been deep-fried.
The new school dinner, designed to keep you thinner,*
Promotes a healthy body and mind,
And with better eating habits
We're all becoming quite refined!

2. So now we dine on soup of the day,
Lightly poached salmon and dauphinoise gratiné,
Not forgetting those asparagus tips.
Yes it's only haute cuisine
That's getting past our lips.
The new school lunch packs a mighty punch,
And is really causing a stir,
'Cause for very little money
We're all eating cordon bleu!

3. We used to find so unpalatable
The very thought of a fruit or vegetable,
Now we're glad to say that's all in the past.
But this food revolution,
How long can it last?
The new school meal, it's a healthier deal
But we're not as fit as we could be............
'Cause at weekends we still pig out
On Burger King and KFC!

* *alternative lyric if you have any children who may be uncomfortable about their weight:*
The new school dinner, well it's a real winner,

## *Continuity Scene*

***Emma*** ~ I'll tell you one thing I *am* looking forward to about leaving primary school – my mum not being around to spy on me at lunchtimes. Ever since she started as a dinner lady my lunchtime breaks have been miserable.

***Ali*** ~ Oh, come on! It can't be that bad. She's really cool your mum. Everyone says so.

***Rachel*** ~ And it's not as if she's just watching you. With all the things those ladies deal with during lunch hour, I'm surprised she even notices you're there.

***Ben*** ~ They certainly earn their money, don't they.

***Emma*** ~ Oh come off it! How difficult can it be? Honestly, the way my mum goes on about it, you'd think she was a member of some special-operations-secret-service type set-up! As if.............

## *Scene 7*

*(A **TV Theme Tune** plays (CD2 - track 25). Centre-stage is a single dining table, around which four children are finishing their lunch. Standing over them, with intimidating postures, are five dinner ladies/lunchtime supervisors, wearing 'SWAT gear' – see staging suggestions/costumes. A narrator stands to one side.)*

***Narrator*** ~ Betty, Doreen, Gladys, Phyllis, and Audrey are members of a crack law-enforcement unit called the Lunchtime Supervisors. We join them as they try to deal with violent trouble-makers at a dining table.

***Betty*** ~ I'm obliged to inform you that flicking peas is an offence under the Lunchtime Code, subsection 6. Read him his rights, Doreen.

***Child 1*** ~ But it was (name of child 2) who spilled them all over the table. I was only clearing a space to put my drink down.

***Doreen*** ~ You have the right to remain silent, but anything you do say will be taken down and used in evidence. Take them to the slammer, Gladys.

***Child 2*** ~ *(fearfully)* The slammer! What's that? I don't want to go to the slammer!

***Child 1*** ~ Don't worry. It just means we have to face the wall for the next half hour.

***Gladys*** ~ Move it you two, and don't even think about trying to make a break for it.

*(She leads the two children off stage.)*

***Phyllis*** ~ *(to the two remaining children)* We know that you tried to get infants to drink vinegar, but we can't prove it, so we're watching you. Now get outside to play, and remember….*(she points to her eyes then at the children.)*

*(The table is removed and all exit. The ladies then re-enter and stand centrally.)*

***Narrator*** ~ With the dining finished the ladies now have to turn their attention to the 'mean streets', in other words the playground and the field.

**_Audrey_** ~ Ok ladies, it's going to be a tough thirty minutes. Remember, if you get into trouble call for back-up. Is your equipment in good order? *(They each produce a whistle and blow in turn.)* Ok, good luck. And ladies.......be careful out there.

*(Two children, a girl chasing a boy, run in front of the stage then disappear to one side. Betty blows her whistle then jumps down from the stage.)*

**_Betty_** ~ One male and one female suspect exceeding the speed limit, traffic code violation 7b, heading east along the playground. I'm in pursuit.

*(She follows them and disappears to one side. The four remaining ladies agitatedly prowl the stage. A child enters and mimes trying to pull open a locked door. Doreen sneaks up on her from behind.)*

**_Narrator_** ~ It's not long before Doreen discovers an attempted break-in!

*(Doreen blows her whistle at the startled child.)*

**_Doreen_** ~ Put your hands behind your head and move slowly away from the door!

*(Still with her back to Doreen the child raises her hands in alarm.)*

Gaining illegal entry to private property is a felony!

**_Child 3_** ~ B....but I'm d...desperate for the loo. I'm busting!

**_Doreen_** ~ You're bust**ed**! Save the excuses for the judge, Princess. Move it!

*(As Doreen frog marches her off, the girl and boy run back along in front of the stage with a tiring Betty still in pursuit. She blows her whistle then stops to catch her breath as the two children exit on the other side.)*

**_Betty_** ~ I'm still in pursuit, heading west by the playground. All units stand by.

*(She follows and exits. Audrey then blows her whistle and points off stage. Phyllis and Gladys stand next to her to see what she's spotted.)*

**_Narrator_** ~ Suddenly, Audrey is alerted to an incident of gross indecency!

**_Audrey_** ~ Two female suspects, wearing skirts, performing handstands against the wall and exposing their under-garments! I'm going in! Cover me!

**_Phyllis_** ~ We've got your back, Audrey. Call for assistance if you need it.

*(Phyllis and Gladys watch Audrey exit. Three boys enter, one with a football, and stand in front of centre stage. A 'rival' group of three boys, one with a football, enter from the other side and approach them. The groups face each other.)*

**_Narrator_** ~ Within moments Gladys hears word of a gang turf-war being waged on the football pitch! The Yr 5 boys think it's their day to use the goal posts, but the Yr 6 boys think differently. Gladys arrives in the middle of a tense stand-off.

*(Gladys moves between the two groups and blows her whistle. The two groups move closer to each other, Gladys in the middle. She again blows her whistle.)*

**_Gladys_**~ Officer in need of assistance! I repeat, officer in need of assistance!

*(Phyllis bounds down from the stage and joins Gladys. The groups step back.)*

**_Phyllis_** ~ Ok gentlemen, we obviously have a situation here. What's the problem?

**_Child 4_** ~ It's Tuesday. That means it's our turn in the goals today.

**_Narrator_** ~ Part of the supervisor's role is conflict resolution. These ladies are highly trained to defuse such potentially dangerous situations.

*(Phyllis takes the ball from one group, and Gladys takes the ball from the other. Together they kick the balls off in opposite directions.)*

**_Phyllis & Gladys_** ~ Now scram, you punks, before we book you! Go on, scram!

*(The boys run off. The boy and girl Betty is chasing then run back across the front of the stage. Phyllis and Gladys block their path.)*

**_Phyllis & Gladys_** ~ Stop in the name of the law!

*(They stop. Betty staggers on, blowing her whistle. Audrey and Doreen return.)*

**_Betty_** ~ *(huffing and puffing)* You two, hands behind your heads and spread 'em! Secure the suspects, ladies. *(Audrey and Doreen hold one child, while Phyllis and Gladys hold the other.)* So, speeding, running without due care and attention, and failing to stop for an officer. You're looking at a three to five stretch for that little lot!

**_Child 5 & 6_** ~ We were only playing kiss chase.

**_Betty_** ~ Kiss chase! Let me see some i.d. *(She fishes paper from their pockets.)* Ha! Just as I thought! You're in Yr4 and you have to be at least in Yr5 to play kiss chase. Underage kiss-chasing is a federal offence. Ha! Add this to the traffic violations and they're gonna throw away the key. Let's take them in. *(They all exit.)*

**_Narrator_** ~ So, as afternoon school begins these brave and tireless ladies finish their shift, happy in the knowledge that, at least for the time being, school is still a safe place for decent people. And any of you out there who think you are above the law, watch out! These girls mean business!

*(As the **TV Theme Tune** (CD2 - track 25) plays the cast take their places for the next song. Fade the music when all are ready.)*

## Song 7 – _The Lunchtime Frontline_ (CD2 - track 7, lyrics p40)

*(When the song finishes, play **Intro Music** (CD2 - track 18) during which chairs and tables are cleared in preparation for the next scene.)*

## *The Lunchtime Frontline*

1. We're on the lunchtime frontline,
   Preventing lunchtime crime.
   'Cause lunchtime's prime time
   For children stepping out of line.
   *(a whistle blows)*
   Oi, you! Stop flicking peas! Whatever are you thinking?
   And you! Stop telling infants vinegar's for drinking!

2. We're on the lunchtime frontline,
   Preventing lunchtime crime.
   'Cause lunchtime's prime time
   For children stepping out of line.
   *(a whistle blows)*
   Oi, you! Stop hiding people's trainers in the sandpit!
   And you! Stop playing bull dogs! Don't you know we've banned it?

**Middle 8**
   We patrol the dinner hall, the playground and the field.
   For law and order we will make a stance,
   To stop those games of kiss chase, those fisticuffs,
   Those girls doing handstands showing everyone their pants!

3. We're on the lunchtime frontline,
   Preventing lunchtime crime.
   'Cause lunchtime's prime time
   For children stepping out of line.
   *(a whistle blows)*
   Ok! Now lunch is over – time that we retreated.
   Once more we leave the field of conflict undefeated!

Elisha + Maddy 2 verses.

## *Continuity Scene*

**Ali** ~ With this being our last day, I'm going to get everyone to sign my school shirt…in permanent felt-tip pen! My mum can't complain, 'cause it's not as if I'm ever going to wear it again.

**Ben** ~ I can't do that. I'm wearing one of my other shirts today, on account of the fact I keep losing my school shirts when I get changed for after-school clubs.

**Rachel** ~ You should go and ask the caretaker *(Mrs Lee)* if you can have a shuffle through the lost-property. There're hundreds of things in there! I bet a few of your shirts are lurking under some old pairs of socks and pants!

**Emma** ~ Yeah, go and see him *(her She's)*. He's really friendly. He'll help you find your shirt. Mind you, this time of year he's probably the busiest person in school. He'll have a thousand and one things to get sorted, I'll bet…………

## *Scene 8*

*(On the main stage, Jim Fixit enters with his gang of workers. They all wear overalls, but Jim's are distinct. He carries a tool box. The others carry a stepladder, pieces of wood, piping etc.)*

***(Note – if your caretaker/premises officer is female you could change this character's name to perhaps Jemima or Jenny Fixit. You could alternatively use your premises officer's real name in the scene if you want to pay tribute to him/her.)***

**Jim** ~ Hello! My name is Jim Fixit, caretaker. People at school write to me with various maintenance problems they'd like me to sort, from those as straightforward as a flickering light bulb in a classroom, to more serious ones, such as a collapsed ceiling in the head's office. No job's too big or too small! Now, before we read this week's letters, let's meet my skilled crew.

**Chippy** ~ Hi, I'm Chippy, and I'm expert in carpentry and joinery.

**Sparky** ~ Hi, I'm Sparky, and I'll take care of anything electrical.

**Bricky** ~ Hi, I'm Bricky, and I'm a wiz with cement and a trowel.

**Pipes** ~ And I'm Pipes. I sort out those little drips in school. No, not the infants!

**Jim** ~ It's good to have you with me, guys. Ok, let's get on. We've had hundreds of letters begging for help, from which we've short-listed ten. We'll then decide on the one which is the most urgent. That will be the maintenance challenge we'll take on this week? Ok, Chippy, read the first letter.

***(Note – you could change the names of the people that the following letters are from, if the content reminds you of certain individuals in your school!)***

**Chippy** ~ Right, here goes. *(S/he unfolds a letter)* 'Dear Jim, could you please find time to retrieve my sixteen footballs from the roof of the school hall. My dad says my poor accuracy is costing him a fortune, and refuses to buy me any more. Yours, Thomas – Yr4.'

**_Jim_** ~ Well, Thomas, you might be lucky. Let's have another letter, Sparky.

**_Sparky_** ~ *(reading)* 'Dear Jim, can you please install another ten power sockets in the Yr 6 classroom. We find there are not enough for us all to re-charge our mobile phones. As you know, we use our phones throughout the day and their batteries quickly run down, which leaves many of us unable to send text messages during afternoon lessons. Yours, the Yr6 girls.' They've all signed it!

**_Jim_** ~ That is a serious problem, girls. The next letter please, Bricky.

**_Bricky_** ~ *(reading)* 'Dear Jim, I'd be very grateful if you and your team could come and repair my desk, which recently collapsed under the weight of all the dirty coffee cups which I neglected to return to the staff room to be washed. Please hurry - it's difficult marking books on the floor! Yours, Miss Allen – Yr3 teacher.'

**_Jim_** ~ Ooh, Miss Allen, that is unfortunate. Pipes, do you have a letter?

**_Pipes_** ~ I do indeed. *(reading)* 'Dear Jim, please could you have a look at our classroom sink. I think there's a problem with the drains, as we can't seem to get rid of the smell of sour milk. We're certain this is due to our teacher actually pouring sour milk down the plug hole, after it's been sitting on the side all day because she constantly forgets to give it to us at morning break, but we'd like you to check anyway. Yours, Samir – Yr2.'

**_Jim_** ~ Well Samir, we may be coming to sort out your pongy problem, but let's hear some more letters before we decide. Sparky?

**_Sparky_** ~ *(reading)* 'Dear Jim, I recently got a new swivel chair for my office, but I've found it doesn't spin as fast as I'd like it to. I really enjoy a mad ten minutes every hour or so, making myself dizzy, but this new chair just doesn't come up to speed. It may need to be oiled. Please help. Yours, Mrs Harris – Secretary.'

**_Jim_** ~ Well, Mrs Harris, you do sound desperate. Maybe you'll win. But Bricky, another letter first.

**_Bricky_** ~ *(reading)* 'Dear Jim, I'd really appreciate it if you could put an extra window in our classroom, just near where I sit. It's impossible to switch off from what my teacher is saying, and enjoy a good daydream, without a view of the field. I'm finding myself actually paying attention in class, which is ruining my cool image. Please help. Yours, Zak Fratelli – Yr3.'

**_Jim_** ~ Oh dear, Zak! That must be terrible for you. Who knows, maybe we can save your reputation. What does the next letter say, Chippy?

**_Chippy_** ~ *(reading)* 'Dear Jim, please, please, please, please, please, please will you remove the mirror from the Yr5 boys' toilet. Every time they look in it they scare themselves half to death, understandably, and are too much in shock to do any work. I've considered making them wear masks, but this would be too impractical. You are my only hope. Yours, Mr Dixon – Yr5 teacher.'

**_Jim_** ~ I understand, Mr Dixon. I've seen the Yr5 boys – ooooh! Not a pretty sight! Pipes, what's next?

**_Pipes_** ~ Here's a letter from a parent. *(reading)* 'Dear Jim, my boy tells me there are no coat hooks in his cloakroom. He says the reason his coat is always covered in filthy footprints is because the only place he can leave it is on the floor. Is this true? If so I must insist you put up hooks immediately. However, if this is yet another example of the lazy little blighter telling me lies, please accept my apologies for wasting your time. Yours, Mrs Adams - address withheld.'

**_Jim_** ~ I can assure you Mrs Adams, there are adequate coat-hanging facilities in your boy's cloakroom, and yes, this is yet another example of the lazy little blighter telling you lies! We'll ignore that letter I think. Sparky, what have you got?

**_Sparky_** ~ *(reading)* 'Dear Jim, would it be possible to install electric fencing at the bottom of the school field. When I'm on play-time duty I really can't be bothered traipsing all the way down there to stop children squeezing through gaps in the hedge. I'm not asking for anything too high-voltage, just enough to fry their fingertips a little, and deter them from ever trying to get out again. Yours, Miss Baker – Deputy Head.'

**_Jim_** ~ Well, that's certainly one of the most unusual requests we've had, Miss Baker. But you never know….. So Bricky, let's hear the last letter before we decide who to help.

**_Bricky_** ~ 'Dear Jim, please adjust the timer on the school bell so it rings fifteen minutes early on Friday. I've got to get my roots done and Jacques the stylist can only fit me in at 3.30pm. Serge could do it at 4.15 but I don't think he's as good as Jacques, and certainly not as handsome. Thanks in anticipation. Yours, Mrs Goldsmith – classroom assistant.'

**_Jim_** ~ And there we have it. That's all the letters read. Which one is the most deserving cause? *(The audience is encouraged to shout out their favourite.)*

Well I think it's clear who's won. But do you know what…… I think we can fix everyone's problem!

*(Jim dramatically pulls off his overalls to reveal a superhero outfit!)*

**_Bricky, Sparky, Chippy & Pipes_** ~ *(smacking their fists like Robin – Batman's sidekick)* Holy Black and Decker, Jim! Are you serious?

**_Jim_** ~ You bet I am. Come on fellas, we've got work to do!

*(To the drum intro of the next song (CD2 - track 8) the cast take their places to sing.)*

## Song 8 – _Mr Fixit_ (CD2 - track 8, lyrics p44)

*(When the song finishes, play **Intro Music** (CD2 - track 18) )*

# Mr Fixit

*(If your caretaker/premises officer is female simply change the title to 'Mrs Fixit'
and all the 'he/him' lyrics to 'she/her' etc.)*

*(Claps during intro)*

1.　If there's mud on the floor,
　　Or your classroom door
　　Comes off its hinges once more,
　　Or the headteacher's chair
　　Needs some urgent repair,
　　Who will always be there?
　　Well he's a real life superhero,
　　Bet he'd look real good in tights!

**Chorus**　Mrs Lee
　　Hey! Mr Fixit! With your box of tricks,
　　You're never short of jobs to do.
　　So many things need mending, everyone's depending
　　On you! Ooh! Ooh! Ooh!

2.　If your classroom sink
　　Is beginning to stink
　　Because your drain's on the blink,
　　Or you've kicked your football
　　Onto the roof of the hall –
　　It's no problem at all. real life superhero
　　'Cause he's a knight in shining armour,
　　A gleaming ladder in his hands
　　And she looks real good in tights!

**Chorus**
　　Hey! Mr Fixit.......

**Instrumental** *(during which Mr Fixit and crew mime a selection of DIY jobs)*

　　Well he's a real life superhero,
　　Bet he'd look real good in tights!

**Chorus**
　　Hey! Mr Fixit....... x 2

## *Continuity Scene*

**_Rachel_** ~ So, have you guys brought a toy in for the last day? I've not bothered 'cause I always lose bits!

**_Ben_** ~ I've got my Nintendo DS and ten games to go with it.

**_Ali_** ~ And if you're lucky, by the end of the day you might still have ten games to take home!

**_Emma_** ~ *(holding up a long piece of elastic)* I've got this!

**_Ben_** ~ What on earth is that? It looks like a piece of old elastic.

**_Emma_** ~ That's exactly what it is.

**_Ali_** ~ What are you supposed to do with it?

**_Emma_** ~ You and another person stand with it stretched between your open legs, at different heights, and another person does tricks and jumps over and around it.

**_Rachel_** ~ What's the point in that?

**_Emma_** ~ It's great fun! My mum showed me how to play it. She and her friends used to play it all the time when they were young. She says kids today spend too much time on their bottoms playing computer games, and if they played more things like 'elastics' we'd all be a lot better off!

**_Ben_** ~ Eurgh! Just imagine that...............

## *Scene 9*

*(On the main stage, four parents enter, each holding the hand of their child, and either pushing prams, carrying briefcases, shopping baskets etc. They stand centre stage and start fussing over their respective children.)*

**_Parent 1_** ~ Now, have you got your book bag and your dinner money?

**_Child 1_** ~ Yes. And please don't kiss me!

**_Parent 1_** ~ Oh, alright. And look. Here's your conker! I threaded it last night. I'll see you at 3.30. Bye.
*(The child exits swinging a conker.)*

**_Parent 2_** ~ Now, I'll be here to collect your sister after school, but not you. You're going home with Jo to have tea at her house. I've told her mum you mustn't have dairy products, you're allergic to salt and that we only ever give you wholemeal bread. And don't stroke their cat. You know it gives you asthma.

**_Child 2_** ~ *(edging away)* Yes, I know. Can I go now please?

**_Parent 2_** ~ Have you got your conker?

**_Child 2_** ~ *(swiftly exiting swinging a conker)* Yep. See you later.

**_Parent 3_** ~ Now I've done your homework for you, so you should get 20 out of 20. Make sure Mr/Mrs ( name ) marks it today, not next week. I know what he's/she's like. And make sure you bring it back home afterwards then I can check he's/she's marked it properly.

**_Child 3_** ~ Have you got my conker?

**_Parent 3_** ~ Of course. Here it is. It's been baking in the oven all night so it's rock-hard. You're bound to win the tournament with that. Good. Right, see you after school.

*(The child exits swinging a conker)*

**_Parent 4_** ~ *(frantically searching in bag, pram, pockets etc)* Oh! I can't find your packed lunch box! I bet I left it on the kitchen table. Oh, and your trip money! *(double-taking at the pram)* The baby! Where's the baby!

**_Child 4_** ~ Mum, it's ok. I have school lunches *my lunch in my bag*, remember. You paid my trip money last week, and grandma's looking after the baby. Calm down!

**_Parent 4_** ~ Yes, yes, of course. Dear me, what am I like. Oh no! Didn't you say you needed a conker today? I've forgotten your conker! Oh dear!

**_Child 4_** ~ *(swinging a conker)* Mum, calm down. I've got it here. Now remember, you've got a doctor's appointment at ten, you're meeting Auntie Sue for lunch, you're picking up the baby at two thirty, and I'm coming home on the bus *walking*, so you don't need to come back here. Right, I'm going in now. Have a nice day.

*(The child exits and the adults gather for a parental chat.)*

**_Parent 1_** ~ I must say, I was glad to hear that the school's banned those computer games. It's all I can do to drag mine away from the silly thing to feed him/her of an evening, without him/her spending breaktimes at school glued to it as well.

**_Parent 2_** ~ Well according to the newsletter it's all part of this new healthy schools campaign. As well as banning gameboys and nintendos at playtime, they've stopped serving chips *allowing crisps* at lunchtime, organised a 'safe walk to school' group, and have introduced traditional, 'good for you' activities to get some fresh air into the kids' lungs between lessons.

**_Parent 3_** ~ I think it's fantastic that they've organised things like hopscotch competitions, British Bulldog contests and this conkers tournament? I've been putting in the hours, training my lad in preparation for it all.

**_Parent 4_** ~ Letter? What letter was that? I didn't get a letter? Or did I? Was it a yellow one or a white one? Did I stick it to the fridge door? Oh dear me!

**_Parent 1_** ~ Stop fretting. Your ( name ) had his/her conker, remember.

'Goodbye, My Friend' by Andrew Oxspring ♻ Printed on 100% recycled paper

***Parent 4*** ~ Did he/she? Oh yes, that's right. Thank goodness.

***Parent 1*** ~ Like I was saying, I'm all for this healthy schools initiative. Children need to be outside and active. It's just not good for them to be sitting on their bottoms all the time, watching TV or playing those daft computer games.

***Parent 2*** ~ I'd go as far as to say it's dangerous. Think of the harm it does to their bodies just sitting there flicking away for hours on end. I mean, you hear about this health-problem time bomb that's just around the corner.

***Parent 3*** ~ I agree, and what could be better than getting them interested in good old-fashioned, healthy competition based on good old-fashioned, simple games.

***Parent 1*** ~ It fills you with confidence to know that, as well as the educational care of our children, schools are taking a lead in providing wholesome, enriching and safe activities for their free time. Oh look, it's nearly 9.30! I can't stand here chatting. Must be off. See you all at 3.30.

***All*** ~ Oh yes / Things to do / I'll be late for work / See you after school / Have a good day etc. *(They all exit.)*

*(Shortly after, a **School Bell** is heard (CD2 - track 19) signifying the end of the school day. The parents enter again, stand centre stage and greet each other.)*

***Parent 4*** ~ Now was I supposed to be here to collect him/her? Oh, dear me I can't remember. Perhaps I should be at the bus stop!

***Parent 3*** ~ I wonder how the conkers tournament went. I hope he won. He'd better have won, with all the tips I gave him.

***Parent 2*** ~ *(annoyed)* It doesn't matter who won. It's just good to know they've been outside at playtime enjoying something that's good for them.

***Parent 1*** ~ Yes. This is definitely a fresh start for my little (_name_). Healthy body, healthy mind, That's what I say. Ooh look, here comes the head.

*(The parents turn to see a very nervous headteacher enter.)*

***Headteacher*** ~ Errm. Hello everybody. I was…errm…just wondering…if…I… errm…could have a quick word before the…errm…children come out.

*(There is confused muttering from the parents.)*

We had…errm…a conkers tournament this lunchtime, as part of our…errm … initiative to…errm…encourage children to take an interest in… errm…more wholesome, enriching and *(speech marks with fingers)* 'better for you' outdoor playtime activities. You remember? As was stated in the last newsletter?

***All*** ~ Yes?

**_Headteacher_** ~ Errm…well, I must just say that the children thoroughly enjoyed themselves….errm…but it appears we misjudged, and indeed forgot, how wholesome, enriching and…errm…good for you a game of conkers actually is.

**_All_** ~ What do you mean?

**_Headteacher_** ~ I'm really sorry!

*(He/she makes a sharp exit as the children walk back on stage. Each and every one is wearing bandages on the fingers, a sling and a cotton wool eye patch! We see that teeth are missing and there is blood on their t-shirts. The parents gasp in horror.)*

**_Parent 1_** ~ Oh my baby! What have they done to you!?

**_Parent 2_** ~ ( name ), Darling, is that you!? Look at your face!

**_Parent 4_** ~ Oh my goodness!

**_Parent 3_** ~ Well? Did you win?

**_All children_** ~ *(awkwardly mumbling through sore mouths)* We've got letters.

*(The children hand their respective parent a letter. The parents unfold them and read them out loud together.)*

**_All parents_** ~ 'Dear parents, at school today your child suffered a slight bump to the head' *(They look at their children's injuries with that face that says 'that's the understatement of the year', then continue reading.)* Should your child complain of a headache, nausea or soreness it is advised you consult your GP. Thank you.

*(The parents look at each other in disbelief.)*

**_Parent 1_** ~ A slight bump to the head! Look at them all!

**_All parents_** ~ 'PS – Please be aware of our new policy regarding the bringing in of unsuitable playtime games. With immediate effect, the pursuit of dangerous pastimes such as conkers is banned at school. Instead, we recommend children bring in games that are more in keeping with our healthy schools initiative….. such as gameboys and nintendos!

*(Intro Music (CD2 - track 18) Fade out when children are in position to sing.)*

## Song 9 – _Ride Our Bikes_ (CD2 - track 9, lyrics p49)

*(When the song finishes, play **Intro Music** (CD2 - track 18).)*

# *Ride Our Bikes*

1. Way back, before there was such a term as 'health and safety',
   We did much more of those risky things we love, but lately
   They've all been banned, been shelved and canned
   In case we get a bruise or,
   We bump our heads or scratch our legs.
   But left alone we'd choose to…..

**Chorus**

    Ride our bikes, and…yikes! Even try with no hands!
    Go for broke at breaststroke not wearing armbands!
    Graze our knees up trees, and take the knocks!
    And run about without our shoes and socks on!

2. It used to be that snow balls were not frowned upon,
   We'd happily take one on the chin then carry on.
   We'd skid over ice and pay the price
   With frozen hands and feet
   But, full of fresh air, we didn't care,
   It felt like such a treat to…..

**Chorus**

3. How we long for breaktimes playing British Bulldog,
   'All pile on', piggyback jousting and leapfrog.
   And if we come a cropper someone's there
   To rub it better.
   Don't mind the pain, join in again,
   Forget the 'bumped-head letter'.

**Chorus**

## *Continuity Scene*

**_Rachel_** ~ I just thought, Emma, it's Friday – you don't usually catch the bus on a Friday, do you?

**_Emma_** ~ No. It's my mum, you see. She's got her knickers in a twist 'cause someone told her there are only 160 shopping days left 'til Christmas, so she wanted to get into town early. That's why she dropped me off here.

**_Ali_** ~ She's keen! Still, at least you know she's thinking ahead about what to get you!

**_Ben_** ~ Now, there's something I really am going to miss about primary school – Christmas. Decorating the classroom, making hats for Christmas lunch, singing carols…..

**_Rachel_** ~ And the infants' nativity. Don't forget that!

**_Ali_** ~ How could we ever…………

## *Scene 10*

*(A teacher enters centre stage and beckons on 3 angels, who will act as narrators. They stand stage right, grinning, scratching and trying to catch their parents' attention with waves. They speak, as do all the characters, in loud and laboured voices, umming, erring and mispronouncing words in typical infant fashion. Mary and Joseph enter and stand centre. Mary is holding a doll by its feet. When the teacher is happy that all is well she sits on a chair stage left.)*

**_Angel 1_** ~ Mary and Jobus were be…betr…beetrooted to get married. The Angel Gabiul came in a dream to talk to Mary and Jobus.

*(Gabriel enters waving to the audience, suddenly becomes stage struck, and starts to cry. The teacher huffs and moves to him. She comforts him then whispers lines which the child attempts to repeat.)*

**_Gabriel_** ~ Fear not Mary and Joseph…..I have been sended by God….You will be having a baby boy what will be called…..Cheeses. *(The teacher escorts a waving Gabriel from the stage then resumes her seat)*

**_Joseph_** ~ *(to teacher, as realisation dawns)* Miss! (_ name _) is holding the baby, and she's not supposed to 'cause he's not been born yet. *(The teacher motions to Joseph to pass her the doll. He speaks to Mary.)* Give me the baby!

*(He grabs the doll by the head and tries to take it from Mary, who is reluctant to let it go of its feet. A struggle ensues, with each pulling the doll. Its head comes off and Mary starts to cry. The flustered teacher stands, comforts Mary then takes the broken doll back to her chair where she tries unsuccessfully to repair it. She puts the two halves under her chair, then motions to Angel 2 to continue.)*

**_Angel 2_** ~ Mary and Joshua…no…Mary and Jonah….no…Mary and…and….

**_Angels 1 & 3_** ~ *(whispering loudly in smug self-satisfaction)* Jobus!

**_Angel 2_** ~ Yes, Mary and Jobus had to go to Befflyham to get registered for their new taxi because Season or Dusters had decreed it.

**_Mary_** ~ *(bossily)* Joseph, I am heavy with child and must ride on the donkey. Go and get it from the field and bring it here now.

*(Joseph exits and brings on a panto donkey. Mary attempts to mount it but it collapses under her weight. She starts crying and the teacher comes on to comfort her. The donkey separates into its two parts and hobbles off, leaving Mary and Joseph confused. The teacher motions to Angel 3 to keep going.)*

**_Angel 3_** ~ So they arrived at Befflyham, and knocked on the door of the inn.

*(The innkeeper enters carrying a crib, trying to conceal the fact he has an itch. He scratches throughout.)*

**_Innkeeper_** ~ Yes. Who is there?

*(The knock is then heard, throwing everything into confusion.)*

**_Joseph & Innkeeper together_** ~ Can we have a room / Yes. Who is there?

*(They look at each other, then at everyone else.)*

**_Joseph & Innkeeper together_** ~ Can we have a room / Yes. Who is there?

*(The teacher motions to Angel 1 to carry on with the narration.)*

**_Joseph, Innkeeper and Angel 1 together_** ~ Can we have a room / Yes. Who is there? / But the inn was full.

*(The teacher stands and calms the situation, then the action continues.)*

**_Angel 1_** ~ But the inn was full because lots of people had come to Befflyham for the reg..is..ti..fi..cation.

**_Innkeeper_** ~ You must go to the stable and have your baby in there with the horses and the cows. It is clean and comfy. It is warm too.

*(He puts the crib at Mary's feet and exits, still scratching. Mary kneels)*

**_Angel 2_** ~ So Mary had the baby Cheeses in the mangy and wrapped him up in a swa…swa…swobbly bands and laid him on the hay.

*(Mary and Joseph panic because the teacher has the doll. Having been unable to repair it, she brings on only the body and lays it in the crib, to more confused looks. Five shepherds enter and sit at the front of the stage. They continually struggle to make their tea towels sit comfortably on their heads.)*

**Angel 3** ~ In the fields the shepherds were counting their sheeps at night. A heathenly host of angels appeared. The shepherds were afraid.

*(The teacher escorts Gabriel to centre stage, behind the shepherds and in front of Mary and Joseph. The narrating angels move to join him.)*

**All angels** ~ *(all speaking at different speeds)* Don't be afraid, for today in the city of David is born a child called Cheeses. Go and see him and take a sheep.

*(Gabriel exits waving, and the angels move back to their narrating positions. The shepherds split and all walk in different directions, not sure where they should be going. The teacher grabs a crook from the nearest to her and rounds them up like sheep. When together again the irate teacher motions to them to speak.)*

**Shepherds** ~ *(ad-libbing poorly out of sync)* Let's go and see the baby / I'll give him a sheep to keep him warm / we must hurry to Befflyham etc etc.

*(The shepherds gather behind Mary and Joseph. One places a card cut-out of a sheep by Mary, but it won't stand up. The teacher pushes the shepherd aside and tries to bend the sheep sufficiently to make it stand. Repeated attempts fail, and in her exasperation she screws up the sheep and stomps back to her seat. Aghast, the children watch her and forget who should speak next. The Angels start squabbling about whose turn it is. The teacher stands.)*

**Teacher** ~ *(beckoning to the back of the room)* Wise men!

*(Three wise men parade awkwardly to the stage, calling and waving to their parents in the audience. One goes to sit with mum, only to be retrieved by the teacher and pushed to the stage. They stand stage left of Mary and Joseph.)*

**Wise man 1** ~ We have been following a bright star that has led us here. We've got some presents for the baby. Here is mine, it's gold.

*(He presents the gift, which Mary greedily grabs and tosses into the crib)*

**Wise man 2** ~ I've got a present too. It's some fr…fran…frantin…

**Angels 1 and 3** ~ Framklimstent!

**Wise man 2** ~ Framklimstent.

*(He presents the gift, which Mary again grabs greedily. Wise man 3 is nervously signalling to the teacher – he isn't holding anything. Everyone waits in silence.)*

**Mary** ~ Well, wise man 3? What have you brought for my baby?

**Wise man 3** ~ *(upset)* Miss! (_name_) forgot his framklimstent, and told me I had to give him my present for the baby, or else he wouldn't be my friend.

**Teacher** ~ Oh, for goodness' sake!

*(She looks around and sees the doll's head under her chair. She picks it up and throws it at wise man 3. He presents it to Mary.)*

**Wise man 3** ~ I have brought myrrh.

*(Everyone gathers round to form a tableau. Each child fidgets and waves, Mary and Joseph attempt to repair the doll, shepherds rearrange their towels, the donkey re-enters (the back end without costume), the innkeeper's itch is now causing severe discomfort, and the wise men have clearly fallen out with each other. The teacher stands in front of the children, addressing the audience.)*

**Teacher** ~ *(forcing a smile)* Thankyou ladies and ge........ *(the noise from the children is distracting.)* Thankyou. Now, we'd like you to...... *(glancing behind her and trying to conceal the fact she is about to blow her top)* Please join us in our final song of the............ *(forcing an unconvincing smile at the audience)* Please sing along with us in...... *(past the point of no return)* Excuse me one moment ladies and gentlemen. *(She turns to the chattering children and lets go!)* WILL YOU JUST BELT UP AND STAND STILL!

*(The children stare in shock, mouths open. The teacher clenches her fists, screws her eyes up and, seemingly lost in her frustration, begins her tirade)*

SIX WEEKS! SIX RELENTLESS WEEKS OF STICKING SHINY PAPER TO CARDBOARD, SEWING SHEETS, GATHERING TEA TOWELS, CUTTING OUT SHEEP, MAKING HALOS AND STAPLING TINSEL TO EVERYTHING THAT MOVES! AND FOR WHAT? SO YOU LOT CAN STAND THERE SCRATCHING YOURSELVES, WAVING AT THE AUDIENCE, SQUABBLING AND FIDDLING WITH YOUR COSTUMES!

*(She throws down her script)*

I DON'T NEED THIS! I'VE GOT ALL MY FAMILY DESCENDING FOR CHRISTMAS DINNER IN SEVEN DAYS TIME AND I HAVEN'T GOT A TURKEY ! I HAVEN'T PUT THE TREE UP YET! I'VE GOT OVER ONE HUNDRED CARDS TO WRITE AND POST, BUT I'VE PROBABLY MISSED THE POSTAGE DEADLINE! THE LIVING ROOM ISN'T DECORATED! AND CHRISTMAS SHOPPING? HA! THAT'S A JOKE! AND THEN THIS CATASTROPHE! NEVER AGAIN! THAT'S THE LAST T......

*(She slowly opens one eye and notices the stunned silence. She takes three deep breaths and composes herself.)*

Thank you ladies and gentlemen. Please join us for our final song, Silent Night.

## Song 10 – *Silent Night? Not Quite!* (CD2 - track 10, lyrics p54)

*(When the song finishes, play **Intro Music** (CD2 - track 18) during which chairs and tables are re-positioned in preparation for the next scene.)*

# Silent Night? Not Quite!

1.  Silent night, holy night,
    The Angel Gabriel's got stage fright.
    Narrators can't pronounce the names,
    The sheep won't stand up and the acting is lame.
    Mary's flattened the mule,
    It's a typical Christmas at school.

2.  Silent night, holy night,
    Parents weep at the sight.
    Brand new camcorders waved in the air,
    Tear sodden tissues are strewn everywhere.
    "Darling, how lucky we are,
    We've given birth to a star."

3.  Silent night, holy night,
    The shepherds' tea-towels are too tight.
    The innkeeper's eczema* is giving him grief,
    His infinite scratching just beggars belief.
    The baby is missing its head,
    Something St Luke never said.

4.  Silent night, holy night,
    Two wise men are having a fight.
    Not quite a Yuletide atmosphere,
    Key stage 2 can do Christmas next year.
    The teacher's losing her cool.
    Peace on earth? Not at school.

## Continuity Scene

**_Emma_** ~ Hey, you know what happens on the last day? We get to take home all of our art work that's been displayed on the walls.

**_Ali_** ~ None of mine ever got put up on the walls! The teacher said that the best place for them was at home – under my bed!

**_Ben_** ~ And I don't think I ever got to show one of my pictures of assembly. Maybe the teacher thought my strange use of colour and shape was as much a reflection of her ability as mine!

**_Rachel_** ~ Well, you have to understand that what goes on the walls, and what is shown in assembly, is really an advert for the class and its artistic talents! And let's face it, your painting is hardly something you'd want to advertise is it!

**_Ali_** ~ What about the line of thought that says if you can hold a pencil and you can look at something properly, you can draw? I can hold a pencil fine, and there's nothing wrong with my eyesight.

**_Emma_** ~ There are exceptions to every rule, Ali. You and Ben are obviously exceptions to that one.

*(They all laugh)*

## Scene 11

*(The action again moves centre-stage where six children sit at tables. They have English SAT papers in front of them, and look thoroughly fed-up. A teacher is talking to them.)*

**_Teacher_** ~ So remember, if you're going to get three marks for those types of questions what must you do?

**_All children_** ~ *(drearily)* Justify our answer by referring directly to the text.

**_Teacher_** ~ That's right. So, moving on. What about…*(sensing their distraction)* …the multiple choice……..OK, what's wrong?

**_Child 1_** ~ I don't think I can take any more of this!

**_Child 2_** ~ Can't we do something fun, like art or PE? We need a break.

**_Teacher_** ~ Look! You've got SATs in less than a fortnight, and I, for one, am not convinced we're as prepared as we could be.

**_Child 2_** ~ But we've done every single practice paper that exists. We've been on a diet of Maths, English and Science for a whole term. If we don't know it by now we never will. Please can we do something fun?

**_Child 3_** ~ Yeah, you've promised we can do painting for weeks now.

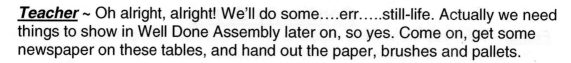

**_Teacher_** ~ Oh alright, alright! We'll do some….err…..still-life. Actually we need things to show in Well Done Assembly later on, so yes. Come on, get some newspaper on these tables, and hand out the paper, brushes and pallets.

**_All Children_** ~ Yes!

*(Newspaper is hurriedly spread over the tables, and a sheet of A3 paper placed in front of each child. **\* (see note on page 57)** The teacher nervously taps his/her fingers and looks at his/her watch. When the tables are covered the children excitedly gather round one table, giggling.)*

**_Teacher_** ~ What is the matter over th…….Oh, I get it. Someone's got an old page 3 of the Sun, have they? Well give it here. It's enough that we have to break from the important stuff without this silliness erupting. Sit in your places!

*(S/he exchanges the sheet of newspaper, and the children excitedly resume their places, eagerly banging and holding their brushes upright, like cutlery when anticipating a meal. S/he looks around the room for a subject to paint, then goes to his/her bag and retrieves a carrier bag of fruit. S/he places an apple and a banana on each table, which the children look at disappointedly.)*

**_Child 3_** ~ Is that it? A bit of old fruit? How are we supposed to get creative inspiration from an apple and a banana?

**_Teacher_** ~ I don't want you to be creative. I want you to get this painting done quickly, neatly and tidily, then we'll have something to show in assembly. We can then clear up and get back to some proper work. Right, off you go.

*(Hurried painting ensues during which the teacher paces around, looking at his/her watch, and closely monitoring the children's efforts. S/he double-takes at a child then pounces over.)*

What on earth do you think you are doing? Stop it at once!

**_Child 3_** ~ I'm painting on the newspaper, to check I've got the right colour mix on my brush before I paint the fruit.

**_Teacher_** ~ You can't do that. What if some of it soaks through the newspaper onto the table? My job's hard enough without getting shouted at by the cleaners. Here let me test the colour. *(S/he sits in the child's place, tests colours and applies them to the picture as the child looks on in frustration.)* There! That's more like it. *(The teacher gets up and the child sits, looking  miserably at the picture.)* Don't touch it! *(S/he moves to the next child.)*

**_Child 4_** ~ *(showing the teacher the picture)* What do you think? I'm really pleased with it. I reckon it's going to be one of the best paintings I've done.

**_Teacher_** ~ Mmmm. I'm not sure you've got the right curve on the banana. Here let me have a go. *(S/he sits in the child's place and works on the picture, as the child looks on in frustration.)* There! That's more like it. *(The teacher gets up and the child sits.)* Don't touch it! *(S/he moves to the next child.)*

**<u>Child 5</u>** ~ This is great fun Mr/Mrs/Miss (<u>name</u>). It's just that I can't seem to get the size right. Can I start again.

**<u>Teacher</u>** ~ No. We haven't got time It's assembly in a minute, and we'll need to start packing up. Here, let me have a go *(S/he sits in the child's place and works on the picture, as the child looks on in frustration.)* There! That's more like it. *(The teacher gets up and the child sits.)* Don't touch it! *(S/he moves to the next child.)*

**<u>Child 6</u>** ~ I'm doing more of an impressionist version of the arrangement. I like to represent the light in an interesting way. Do you like it?

**<u>Teacher</u>** ~ But it looks nothing like what's in front of you! Here, let me have a go *(S/he sits in the child's place and works on the picture, as the child looks on in frustration.)* There! That's more like it. *(The child sits and looks at the picture)* Don't touch it! *(The teacher then addresses the class.)* Now children, it's time to tidy up. I'd like you put things away without making a mess.

**<u>All children</u>** ~ But we've hardly had any time / Is that all we're getting / Year 5 get a whole afternoon / I'm only just getting into it..... etc

**<u>Child 1</u>** ~ What about those of us that haven't finished?

**<u>Teacher</u>** ~ *(looking at watch)* Oh really! Right put up your hand if you've not finished. *(Hands go up from children 1 and 2. The teacher rushes from one to the next, finishing off, and changing the paintings, as the children look on in frustration.)* Now don't touch them. Now, come on everyone. A quick tidy-up please, and then into assembly.

*(The children, urged by the teacher, clear things away. They look very disgruntled. When ready, the teacher leads them, each carrying their paper (painted side to their chests, blank side to the audience) to stand at the front of the stage, as if to show their work to an assembly audience. The teacher stands to the side of the line of children, and addresses the hall.)*

Well, year 6 have been working extremely hard on some still-life pictures. It's taken a long time and a lot of concentration and effort, but I think you'll agree that each one has produced a lovely picture. And, it was all their own work.

*(The teacher smiles awkwardly, as the children in turn reveal identical paintings of an apple and banana. **\* Note** - These have been photocopied and painted in advance, and put picture-side down in the children's places when setting out the newspaper, without the audience seeing them.)*

*(**Intro Music** (CD2 - track 18) Fade out when children are in position to sing.)*

## *Song 11 – <u>Arty Party</u>* (CD2 - track 11, lyrics p58)

*(When the song finishes, play **Intro Music** (CD2 - track 18) during which chairs and tables are re-positioned in preparation for the next scene.)*

# ***Arty Party***

1.  We've got the paint out, the brushes too,
    The shiny paper, the pots of glue,
    But the teacher doesn't look impressed
    Because the chances are we'll make a terrible mess.
    She's gonna get it in the neck
    From the caretaker, but what the heck.
    We've waited so long, now it's finally here,
    We get to do art for the first time this year.
    We're so happy – hip hip hooray!

2.  We've got sheets of newspaper to stop
    Paint splashing the table-top.
    But the teacher's terrified that someone
    Might find an old page 3 of the Sun.
    She's watching our every move
    For things of which she doesn't approve,
    But we've got the chance to create at last,
    We'll be colouring in! We'll be having a blast!
    And we're happy – hip hip hooray!

3.  A bit of still-life, a landscape or two,
    It's not quite Monet, but hey, it'll do.
    And if it's not displayed prominently,
    And I never get to show it in assembly,
    At least I've had some time, at last,
    Away from boring practice SATs
    And though it seems, quite possibly,
    I won't do art again 'til key stage 3
    I'm still happy – hip hip hooray!

    Oh I'm so happy, yes I'm so happy,
    Hip hip hooray!

## *Continuity Scene*

**_Ben_** ~ Rachel, how come you're little brother isn't with you today?

**_Rachel_** ~ Oh, he coughed once in the night so Mum's keeping him off! He knows how to wind her round his little finger. There's nothing wrong with him!

**_Ali_** ~ They're all the same, these infants. They know they're 'precious', so they play on it for an easy ride! They get away with murder just by being cute!

**_Emma_** ~ You can say that again. I reckon they're all evil geniuses, who are playing the rest of us for fools! They're exactly the same at school……..

## *Scene 12*

*(The action again crosses to the main stage where two parents enter, one from either side of the stage, holding the hand, and carrying school bag of an infant-aged child in a coat. The children speak to their parents in typical infant voices.)*

**_Child 1_** ~ Mummy! Mummy! There's Jack! Pwease can I go and pway wiv him?

**_Child 2_** ~ Daddy! Daddy! It's Katy wiv her mummy.

*(The two children meet and stand stage left, while the parents stand and chat stage right, out of earshot but keeping a watchful eye.)*

**_Parent 1_** ~ They grow up so fast don't they? She's already using cutlery.

**_Parent 2_** ~ Tell me about it. He's into everything. Gone are the days when he'd be satisfied with an hour of Teletubbies.

**_Parent 1_** ~ Yes, but they're still sweet at this age, aren't they, and so innocent.

*(They stare adoringly across at their children and wave. The children smile and give a cute wave back. The parents resume their conversation, while the children proceed to speak to each other in mature, sophisticated voices.)*

**_Child 1_** ~ I read a fascinating article in the Guardian yesterday about our EU rebate. I tell you, it's a political time bomb.

**_Child 2_** ~ Yes, I'm familiar with the piece, although I only managed to get a third of the way through it before I had to hide it under my mattress, when I heard mother ascending the stairs to switch off my Winnie the Pooh lamp. I detest that lamp – I find it so patronising and demeaning.

**_Child 1_** ~ I know. For some reason, known only to them, my parents think I enjoy Thomas the Tank Engine, and so all my bedroom furniture is emblazoned with his infantile, gurning expression…….Oooh! They're coming over.

*(The parents approach and the children adopt a coy and wide-eyed expression.)*

**_Parent 1_** ~ Come on. Mummy take your coat off and change your shoes.

**_Parent 2_** ~ And Daddy help his little soldier too.

*(The parents take off their respective child's coat, then kneel before them, backs to the audience, and take off their shoes and replace them with plimsolls taken from the school bags. The children are still standing facing the audience. They are able to talk to each other without their kneeling parents hearing.)*

**Child 2** ~ You know, I find this changing of shoes somewhat tiresome.

**Child 1** ~ Regulations are regulations. Where would society be without them?

*(Holding the coats and outdoor shoes, the parents stand up next to their child.)*

**Parent 1** ~ There we are Munchkin, all ready for school.

**Child 1** ~ *(in an infant voice)* Fank you Mummy. Pwease will you bwing my bag and coat and shoes in da woom. Day are too heavy for me to cawwy.

**Parent 1** ~ Of course Munchkin.

*(Parent 1 and Child 1 exit. Child 1 gives Child 2 a knowing wink.)*

**Parent 2** ~ There you are Tiger. You're ready too.

**Child 2** ~ Daddy, pwease will you come in wiv me and tell Mrs/Miss ( name ) dat it isn't my fault dat I didn't do my weading last night. Pwease Daddy!

**Parent 2** ~ Of course I will. Come on.

*(Parent 2 and Child 2 exit. Child 2 gives the audience a knowing wink. Straight away a teacher, carrying 4 pencils and 4 sheets of paper, leads a group of eight children, including Child 1 and Child 2, back onto the empty stage. A teaching assistant brings up the rear carrying a set of 5 reading books. While the children sit cross legged in a line at the front of the stage, backs to the audience, the two adults bring two tables from the back, and place each one at opposite sides of the stage. Five chairs are positioned round each of the tables. The teacher then sits on another chair in the middle, facing the children and audience, and the assistant sits on the middle chair at one of the tables.)*

**Teacher** ~ Good morning, children.

**Children** ~ *(Speaking the traditional whiney, laboured reply)* Good morning Mrs/Miss ( name ). Good morning evwy-one.

**Teacher** ~ Thank you. Now, let me explain what will be happening this morning. The blue group will be working with me doing some writing, while Mrs ( name ) will take the yellow group to do some reading. We need to think about….

*(Her voice fades but she carries on mouthing and gesturing as if still addressing the class, but silently, so we can hear the following conversation between the children. Child 3 and Child 4 turn round on their bottoms to face the audience.)*

**Child 3** ~ It's reading for us then. *(sarcastically)* I wonder what literary masterpieces we have in store?

**_Child 4_** ~ I can't wait to tackle the surrealistic subplot of 'Elmer The Elephant.'

**_Teacher_** ~ *(noticing them)* Ahem! What are you two chatting about?

**_Child 3_** ~ I said I want to sit next to ( name ) for because s/he's my fwend.

**_Teacher_** ~ Well, I suppose so, if that's OK with Mrs ( name ). *(The assistant nods)* Good. Well that's lovely. Would the blue group join me at this table…..

**_Assistant_** ~ And would the yellow group join me at this table.

*(Children 1 and 2 sit one side of the assistant at her table, Child 3 and 4 on her other side. Reading books are given out and they begin a group read. Children 5, 6, 7, and 8 sit with the teacher, who gives them a pencil and some paper.)*

**_Teacher_** ~ Now, blue group, today we will be writing sentences about things we like to do in our spare time. *(to child 5)* What do you like to do?

**_Child 5_** ~ I like to wide my bike outside in da stweet.

**_Teacher_** ~ Lovely. *(to child 6)* And how about you ( name )?

**_Child 6_** ~ Sometimes I bake bwead wiv my Mummy.

**_Teacher_** ~ Lovely. *(to child 7)* And you ( name )?

**_Child 7_** ~ I pway wiv my puppy in da garden. We woll awound. It's gweat fun.

**_Teacher_** ~ Lovely. Puppies are fun, aren't they. *(to child 8)* And you ( name )?

**_Child 8_** ~ I like pwaying wiv my cars .

**_Teacher_** ~ Good. Now, with your pencils, in your neatest writing, I'd like you all to write down what you've told me, and then you can draw a picture to go with it.

*(She crouches by child 8 to assist. Children 5, 6 and 7 have a sneaky chat.)*

**_Child 5_** ~ That's actually a complete fabrication. I hate riding my bike. It's such a pointless exercise. My spare time is, in fact, taken up designing websites for some quite exclusive corporate clients.

**_Child 6_** ~ I never bake bread and neither does my mum. I'm too busy with my Open University course in applied mathematics. It takes it out of me, I tell you, which is why I come here – to recharge my batteries.

**_Child 7_** ~ And I've been up all night trying to crack the Times crossword. I'm exhausted. I could do with getting my head down, never mind writing sentences.

**_Teacher_** ~ What are you three chatting about?

**_Child 5, 6 & 7_** ~ We don't know what to wite. Will you wite it for us and den we can copy it?

**Teacher** ~ *(sighing)* What, again? OK, but this is the last time. Tomorrow you try it on your own. Pass me your books. Now, ( name ), what was your sentence?

*(She writes in each of their books and the children relax in their chairs, smiling contentedly as the action moves to the reading table.)*

**Assistant** ~ *(slightly exasperated)* OK, ( name ), let's try again. From page one.

**Child 3** ~ O...O...On...On....e....d...da...da...y.  I can't wead it!

**Assistant** ~ *(sigh)* Never mind, Dear. Right, *(to child 1)* Katy, you have a go.

*(As the assistant turns to focus on Child 1, Child 3 relaxes and produces a copy of the Economist which s/he and Child 4 flick through together behind her back.)*

**Child 1** ~ O...O...On...On....e....d...da...da...y.  I can't wead it!

**Assistant** ~ *(sigh)* Not to worry *(turning to Child 4)* ( name ), how about you?

*(As she turns back to Child 3 and 4's side, they quickly hide the Economist and pretend to be looking at the reading book. Child 1 then relaxes and produces a copy of National Geographic, which she and Child 2 casually flick through.)*

**Child 4** ~ O...O...On...On....e....d...da...da...y.  I can't wead it!

**Assistant** ~ *(sigh)* Right, this just isn't working. *(calling to the teacher)* Mrs/Miss ( name ), may I have a word.

**Teacher** ~ Yes, one moment Mrs ( name ). *(to the children)* Just, put your pencils down. Don't do any more. I'll be back in a second.

*(The two adults meet in the middle. The children watch them)*

**Assistant** ~ How's it going with you? Mine are really struggling.

**Teacher** ~ It's the same over there. I don't know what's wrong. You'd think after three terms they'd be showing some progress. So, what do you say? The usual?

**Assistant** ~ Might as well. Ok children, who'd like to play in the sand tray?

*(They exit and all the children relax back in their chairs with a contented smile.)*

*(**Intro Music** (CD2 - track 18) Fade out when children are in position to sing.)*

## Song 12 – *I Wish I was An Infant Again* (CD2 - track 12, lyrics p63)

*(When the song finishes, play **Intro Music** (CD2 - track 18) during which chairs and tables are re-positioned in preparation for the next scene.)*

# I Wish I Was An Infant Again

1.  I wish I was an infant again,
    Yes I wish I was an infant again.
    Things were less complicated,
    It seemed so simple then.
    I'd play with sand and water
    And rarely pick up a pen.
    Oh, to re-live the good times,
    I wish I was an infant again.

2.  I want to go back to Key Stage One,
    Yes I want to back to Key Stage One.
    The grown ups would tie my laces
    Whenever they came undone.
    At home time they'd pack my book bag
    And help me put my coat on.
    But now I'm left to struggle, oh
    I want to go back to Key Stage One.

3.  I wish I could be five years old,
    Yes I wish I could be five years old.
    'Cause the teachers don't blow a gasket
    When you don't do as you're told.
    They chastise you so sweetly
    And never scowl or scold,
    But now I've come of age they fly into a rage
    Like a banshee who's possessed! I'm really not impressed.....
    I wish I could be five years old.

*[handwritten annotations:]*

CBBC
'5'Again

Big Brother
chair

Making mince meat - hazards of grater

Aiming for Arthur Pender rubber/ruler hit Mrs Renyard on the bottom

When I was at the front of the line Matthew pulled my trousers down.

Josh still misses Lightning McQueen from the bush.

Bad jokes

Construction time

## Continuity Scene

**Rachel** ~ Do you reckon we'll able to watch DVDs today? You know, in between playing games, getting our shirts signed and collecting our artwork?

**Ali** ~ I hope so. I've brought a couple of choice titles, just in case!

**Ben** ~ Not those ones we watched round yours the other night! The teacher will never let you put those on!

**Ali** ~ Oh, what she doesn't know won't hurt her! Anyway, all the adults will be far too busy today to worry about what we're watching.

**Emma** ~ I wouldn't be too sure, you know. They have to be very careful these days, that what they show us doesn't cause us any distress, or lead us to behave inappropriately!

**Rachel** ~ Well, that's all the interesting stuff out of the window then. I wonder what televisual delights she'll have in store for us………….

## Scene 13

*(The action again moves centre stage, to where the furniture is set up similar to scene 11. A television and video/DVD player are positioned so the audience can't see the screen. A stepladder stands against one wall. As the children sit at the tables chatting, a flustered teacher enters, laden down with painted pictures and old display material, which he/she dumps on one of the tables.)*

**Teacher** ~ Ok, listen everybody. As it's the last day I've got a lot to organise, so if you're sensible you can amuse yourselves this morning.

**Child 1** ~ ( name ) has brought in some videos and DVDs. Can we watch one?

**Teacher** ~ *(climbing the stepladder)* I told you, I don't mind what you do as long as you're sensible, and I'm not interrupted.

*(The teacher turns away from the children and attends to a wall display. The children excitedly gather round the collection of videos and DVDs.)*

**Child 1** ~ Cool. Go on ( name ), put on 'Alien Blood Bath'. My sister says it's a classic. There's a body count of 25 in the first minute!

**All Children** ~ Cool!

**Child 2** ~ Ok, here goes! I hope you're sitting comfortably.

*(He/she puts the film in the machine and the children sit close to the TV. The teacher is still up the stepladder. The children react with excitement to the TV.)*

**Child 3** ~ Wow. He got blasted right through the window.

**All Children** ~ Cool!

**Child 4** ~ Eurgh. The alien tore his guts out. Look at all the blood!

**All Children** ~ Awesome!

**Child 5** ~ Did you see that? She fell onto a massive spike…and she's still alive!

**All Children** ~ Gasp!…………Eurgh!

**Child 6** ~ Not anymore she's not!

**All Children** ~ Wicked!

*(The teacher descends the ladder to investigate. On seeing the TV screen his/her jaw drops.)*

**Teacher** ~ Oh my goodness! Turn it off! Turn it off this instant! What on earth are you watching?! *(S/he rushes to the TV and switches it off, to the groans and protests of the children.)* Where did you get this rubbish from?

**Child 2** ~ It's my brother's, Mr/Mrs/Miss (_name_). But it's not rubbish. It's amazing. You just missed a bit where…….

**Teacher** ~ Yes, thank you (_name_). Well, it is rubbish, and I cannot let you watch that sort of thing in school. It's vulgar. Every other word is a swear word! And the violence! The violence is intolerable. Now, where's that video I brought in? Ah yes. *(The teacher takes a tape from a bag, ejects 'Alien Blood Bath', turns the TV on and inserts the new tape.)* Right, if you're going to watch the TV then at least it can be educational. This is a programme I recorded off BBC2 last night. I've not seen it yet but I've been told it's superb. It's called 'Shakespeare In Pieces'. It's lots of different scenes from the wonderful plays of William Shakespeare. You can watch it quietly while I carry on over here.

*(The children tut and slouch, watching the screen with grumpy expressions.)*

*(As **Tudor music** plays (CD2 - track 26) three actors in Shakespearean costume enter and stand in front of the stage, to act out a section from a play. The children still watch and react to the TV, as if seeing this action on the screen.)*

**Portia** ~ Why, this bond is forfeit, and lawfully, by this, Shylock can claim his pound of flesh to be, by him, cut off from nearest the merchant's heart!

**All Children** ~ *(suddenly sitting up and looking interested.)* Cool!

**Bassanio** ~ No, Shylock shall have my flesh, blood, bones and all, ere thou shalt lose for me one drop of blood.

**All Children** ~ Wicked!

**Shylock** ~ Now I whet my blade to cut the pound of flesh from this bankrupt!

**All Children** ~ Go on! Go on! Do it! Do it!

*(The TV action freezes. The teacher turns and looks nervously at the children.
**Tudor music** plays (CD2 - track 26) and two more actors replace the first three.)*

**King** ~ All hail Macdonald.

**Macdonald** ~ *(pulling a head from a sack!)* Hail King, for so thou art. Macbeth is
dead! Behold where he stood, the usurper's head!

**All Children** ~ He cut off his head! Awesome!

**Teacher** ~ *(coming down the stepladder.)* Errm, actually children I think Yr 1
need the TV, so I'll just eject the…

**All Children** ~ No! No! Leave it. Look, here comes some more!

*(**Tudor music** plays once more (CD2 - track 26) and two more actors replace the
previous two.)*

**Pistol** ~ *(wielding a sword)* Yield cur, for I will fetch the rim out of your throat!

**All Children** ~ Eurgh! Brilliant!

**Soldier** ~ Is it impossible to escape the force of your arm?

**Pistol** ~ By envy's hand and murder's bloody axe, unless you give me crowns,
mangled shalt thou be by this sword!

**Soldier** ~ I have nothing.

**Pistol** ~ Then you are slain! *(With piercing cries the soldier is hacked down.)*

**All Children** ~ Wow! Cool! Awesome!

**Teacher** ~ *(fighting his/her way through the children to get to the TV)* Right!
That's it children. Sorry!

*(The teacher ejects the tape, blowing heavily with relief, as if having just de-
fused a bomb that was due to go off any second. The children are distraught.)*

**Child 6** ~ But what are you doing Mr/Mrs/Miss ( name )?

**Teacher** ~ *(inserting another video)* What do you think I'm doing? I'm putting
'Alien Blood Bath' back on!

*(**Intro Music** (CD2 - track 18) Fade out when children are in position to sing.)*

## Song 13 – Yucky Stuff *(CD2 - track 13, lyrics p67)*

*(When the song finishes, play **Intro Music** (CD2 - track 18))*

# *Yucky Stuff*

1. No, we're not into niceties.
   We've not got time for those PGs.
   We want to see a car chase
   Star ships exploding in space,
   A little bit of action please.
   Your average kid just wants t' see some big hairy monster
   With an appetite to match!
   It's thrilling when 'goo' is spilling
   We just can't get enough
   Of all that really yucky stuff.

2. Those golden oldies are a bore,
   And costume dramas make us snore!
   What's cool and oh so groovy
   Is zombies in a movie
   Giving aliens 'what for'!
   Don't want no 40's classic, give us something Jurassic,
   With teeth as sharp as razor blades!
   You can't beat a huge meat eater,
   We just can't get enough
   Of all that really yucky stuff.

3. Turn out the lights, sit in the dark.
   This one's about a killer shark!
   We are already smitten
   'Cause some poor bloke's been bitten,
   And it's left a pretty nasty mark!
   But when it all starts gushin' we'll hide behind a cushion
   Not quite as brave as we believed.
   We want Tom and Jerry 'cause it's not so scary,
   We've had about enough
   Of all that really yucky.......
   That filthy, slimy, mucky......
   All that really yucky stuff.

## Continuity Scene / Scene 14

**Rachel** ~ Listen! Can you hear that? I think the bus is coming! I'd recognise that clatter of rusty metal and the sound of bad gear-changing anywhere!

**Emma** ~ Well about time too! How long as that been? We're bound to be late now, and on our last day!

**Ali** ~ I don't know what you're complaining for!

**Ben** ~ *(dejectedly)* I wish the bus hadn't come at all.

**Ali** ~ Yeah, me too! I'd much rather….

**Ben** ~ No, Ali. Not for the same reasons as you. It's just that if the bus hadn't picked us up, we wouldn't have to have a last day at school.

**Rachel** ~ What do you mean, Ben?

**Ben** ~ Oh, I don't know. I suppose with all this talk of the weird and wonderful people we've met there, and the unbelievable things we've done, I don't want to leave. I don't want to have a last day.

**Emma** ~ I know how you feel. I don't want to go either. It only seems like yesterday that we started school, and I can't believe it's already time to move on.

**Rachel** ~ I know, but we can't stand still, guys. There's a big and exciting world out there, and we need to go and grab it with both hands.

**Ben** ~ I guess you're right. It is going to be an exciting next few years. Who knows what's going happen? But I'll never forget our little school. It's been like a friend, and now we have to say goodbye.

**Ali** ~ Well, you can't say goodbye properly from a bus stop, can you? So come on, you big softie! Let's get on this bus, and have a fantastic last day at school! *(holding his hand up to stop the bus)* Are you all ready?

**Ben, Emma & Rachel** ~ Yeah!

**Ali** ~ Then let's go!

*(The four move to the main stage to join the rest of the cast for the final song.)*

### Song 14 – <u>Goodbye My Friend</u> (CD2 - track 14, lyrics p69)
### <u>'Til The End</u> (CD2 - track 15, lyrics p70)
### <u>Wonderful Days</u> (CD2 - track 16, lyrics p71)
### <u>Every Single Step Of The Way</u> (CD2 - track 17, lyrics p72)

# THE END

# *Goodbye My Friend*

**1.** Another summertime has come,
Those endless days just filled with fun.
And yet this summertime will be
A little different for me.
Though many brightly shining lights are beckoning,
Right here, right now will always be special to me.
And so it's….

**Chorus**
Goodbye my friend, it's not the end,
How could it be when we've got
Such memories to set us free
When we find being grown up isn't all that it's cracked up to be.

**2.** Here's where I learned to use a pen
And count in multiples of ten.
Here's where I learned of foreign lands,
And how to swim without arm-bands.
Though opportunity is knocking at my door,
Right here, right now, is what really matters to me.
And so it's….

**Chorus**
Goodbye my friend……..

**3.** And, who knows, when we're old and grey
We'll raise a glass to yesterday.
We'll talk of characters long-gone
And wonder how they're getting on.
And I hope that our paths will cross again some day,
'Cause right here, right now, will always be precious to me.
And so it's….

**Chorus x 2**
Goodbye my friend……..x2

# 'Til The End

1.  As I'm standing here,
    My whole life in front of me,
    The future's far from clear,
    And I guess what will be will be.
    But looking back I'm sure
    I could not have wished for more,
    The days rolled by so easily.

*[handwritten: Nicholas 'Graduation Speech']*

**Chorus**

> If I could have my time again
> I wouldn't change a thing.
> The moments spent with you my friend,
> Are with me forever.
> I'll hold and I'll treasure each one 'til the end.

2.  As we're standing here,
    Shoulder to shoulder, side by side,
    My every hope and fear
    I would willingly confide.
    'Cause there's no-one, I'm sure,
    I could have trusted more,
    Or who I'd rather walk beside.

*[handwritten: Kath, Jas, Abi / Molly, Lucy, Adi / Elisha, Holly, Maddy / Ella.]*

**Chorus**

> If I could have……..

3.  Every day was an adventure,
    Every day brought something new.
    We shared the ups and downs together.
    Oh, how we learned and how we grew.

*[handwritten: All girls + anyone who wants to sing]*

**Chorus**

> If I could have…….. x2

*[handwritten: All stand.]*

# *Wonderful Days*

1.  When you're king of the pond you're in
    No fish are as big as you.
    It won't be long 'til we move on
    To oceans deep and blue.
    And though we're fond of our little pond
    And sad to say goodbye,
    A piece of you goes with us on our way.

**Chorus**

Wonderful days,
Such happy times we've spent with you.
And some might say
These are the best days of our lives.

2.  Memories of muddy knees
    And milk drunk through a straw.
    A shoe or two found in the loo,
    Coats on the cloakroom floor.
    We'd take delight in a snowball fight,
    And bulldogs on the field,
    And take the bumps and bruises with a smile.

**Chorus**

Wonderful days……..

**Bridge**

Waking up at 4.15
To make sure Santa Claus had been,
And Easter eggs were worth their weight in gold.
My first time off the diving-board,
Races I've won, the goals I've scored,
Things to bring a smile when I grow old.

**Chorus**

Wonderful days…….. x2

## *Every Single Step Of The Way*

1. Sometimes we win, sometimes we lose,
   Sometimes we just watch from the sidelines.
   Sometimes we run, sometimes we choose
   To stay and wait for the sun to shine.
   Whatever each new day brings,
   We can weather the storm together.
   And we'll embrace all those things
   That life puts in our way.

2. One moment I feel ten feet tall,
   The next I'm hiding in the shadows.
   One moment my back's to the wall
   The next my strength of spirit grows.
   So many twists and turns
   Beset our travels as life unravels.
   So many lessons learned,
   But the one I hold most dear is......

**Chorus**

Every time that I laugh or cry
You're with me, sharing every moment.
You stick around through my ups and downs,
Beside me every single step of the way.

**Instrumental**

3. And now we wave a fond goodbye,
   And now we leave this all behind,
   And now we spread our wings and fly,
   So uncertain of what we'll find.
   When we reach our journey's end
   We'll look back gladly on all we had.
   We will remember good times, my friend,
   And how we used to say.....

**Chorus**

Every time......x2

# *STAGING AND PRODUCTION SUGGESTIONS*

The action in 'Goodbye, My Friend' alternates between a bus stop (where the continuity scenes are set) and other situations in or around a school, with the exception of scene 4. We suggest our usual staging layout similar to this.....

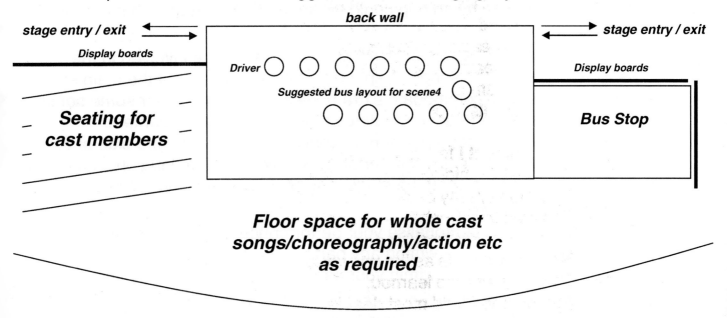

**Audience**

- ***Scenery -*** On the display boards behind the smaller stage, paint scenery to represent the bus stop. A post with a 'Bus Stop' sign would look effective. If you're feeling especially adventurous, why not create a 'roof' attached to the display boards at the back, and held up on posts at the two front corners. A simple trestle bench could be used for the continuity characters to sit on. The back wall behind the main stage could display large letters spelling out 'Goodbye, My Friend' or whatever name you choose to give to your production. Large paintings depicting memorable scenes and characters from school life, or those referred to in the script, would be in keeping with the theme of your production. Alternatively, a large photograph of each child would add to the sense of occasion.

- ***Furniture -*** The furniture for the scenes on the main stage need only be standard school tables and chairs. Work out an arrangement for each scene that suits your space, then practice moving them in and out of position during the intro music between scenes. We have illustrated a suggested layout for chairs to represent a bus in scene 4.

- ***Props -*** To keep things simple, all props are things that can be found in and around school, in most cupboards and on most shelves. For the dining scene (6) you will need to borrow cutlery and table settings that are slightly more glamorous than your school kitchen will be able to provide. For scene 9, if no conkers have survived until the summer term, simply use balls of modelling clay attached to lengths of string.

- **Costume** – As with the props, costume requirements have been kept to a minimum. Those playing children should simply wear normal school clothes, while those playing teachers or parents should take inspiration from their own families and the staff at school. Ask your kitchen staff nicely for spare tabards and 'whites' for scene 6. Overalls for scene 8 could be borrowed from home, and a peaked cap could be adapted to represent that of a bus driver in scene 4.

- **Use of Space** - The whole cast will probably want to be involved in the performance of all the songs. A space on the floor in front of the main stage could be used to accommodate extra bodies. In this space, for some songs, the cast could perform dance routines or act out the lyrical content.
A seating area for resting performers could be allocated to one side of the stage. This lets them enjoy the performance as part of the audience, allows easy movement on and off the stage, and of course eliminates the need for back-stage supervision.

- **Content** – You can personalise your performance by adding or changing character names, and re-writing any parts of the script to relate more closely to the things that happen within your particular school. You may find your children and staff are inspired to recall and write about other humorous or memorable events and characters from their own experiences. This production is perfect for incorporating your own creative ideas. Different songs that the children know and enjoy could replace, or be added to those on the CD. Don't feel restricted – make the show your own.

- **Audience seating** - Finally, we suggest the audience be seated at tables (cabaret style), and encouraged to bring drinks and nibbles of their choice. If this is being performed as a leavers' concert, a relaxed party atmosphere will really make the evening go with a swing, and give parents, staff and children something to remember for a long time.

Please email, phone or write to us if you have any production queries at all, and we'll be more than happy to help.

As always, we hope you have fun and enjoy yourselves with this production – that's the only reason it's been written!